It Wasn't Roaring, It Was Weeping

It Wasn't Roaring, It Was Weeping

Interpreting the Language of Our Fathers
Without Repeating Their Stories

LISA-JO BAKER

Convergent Books
New York

Published in the United States by Convergent Books, an imprint of Random House, a division of Penguin Random House LLC, New York.

Convergent Books is a registered trademark and the Convergent colophon is a trademark of Penguin Random House LLC.

LIBRARY OF CONGRESS CATALOGING-IN-PUBLICATION DATA
Names: Baker, Lisa-Jo, author.
Title: It wasn't roaring, it was weeping / Lisa-Jo Baker.
Other titles: It was not roaring, it was weeping
Description: First edition. | New York, NY: Convergent Books, [2024]
Identifiers: LCCN 2023048684 (print) | LCCN 2023048685 (ebook) |
ISBN 9780525652861 (hardback) | ISBN 9780525652878 (ebook)
Subjects: LCSH: Baker, Lisa-Jo. | Baker, Lisa-Jo—Family. | Pretoria
(South Africa)—Biography. | Pretoria (South Africa)—Social life and
customs—20th century. | Fathers and daughters—South Africa—
Pretoria. | Women—Maryland—Biography. | Maryland—Biography.
Classification: LCC DT2403.23.B35 A3 2024 (print) | LCC DT2403.23.
B35 (ebook) | DDC 968.22/7506092 [B]—dc23/eng/20240126
LC record available at https://lccn.loc.gov/2023048684
LC ebook record available at https://lccn.loc.gov/2023048685

Hardback ISBN: 978-0-525-65286-1
Ebook ISBN: 978-0-525-65287-8

Printed in Canada on acid-free paper

convergentbooks.com

2 4 6 8 9 7 5 3 1

First Edition

Book design by Virginia Norey

This book is for my father, Peter Rous.
And for my motherland, South Africa.

Contents

AUTHOR'S NOTE TO THE READER

My brothers make movies for a living, and they often say that the person who gets to tell a story publicly sets the story in cement. I am very aware that this is my version of events that I shared with a family and a nation. And while mine is set down in the cement of these pages, the bigger story is still a living, breathing family tree. I love this tree like I love jacaranda trees—that is to say, with my whole heart.

I have written the part of the story that is mine. And where it intersected with people and places and history, great care has been taken to be as accurate and as honest as possible. My father has read every word of this book and throughout the four years of its creation has given me the great gift of remembering alongside me. To trust a child with your story, from *her* perspective, is no small thing. The same could be said for trusting a sibling to tell your shared childhood. Mine have granted me trust and grace that I don't take lightly. No details or events have been altered, but the perspective is uniquely mine. And a handful of names have been changed to honor the privacy of these people: Nicole, Grant Forest, Gerry Jabulani, Onthou, Kleinboy, Heather, Patrice, Rita, Monique, and Daria.

Language is an important character in this book. South Africa has *twelve* national languages; I appreciate the weight of history that words hold and the power they have to shape new futures. I have listened to the conversations taking place in both South Africa and the United States regarding capitalization of racial designations. For the purposes of this book, I have capitalized Black and White to reclaim these words from a segregated history, to ensure that there is no one group defined as the norm against which all the rest are other, and to honor our shared humanity.

The title of this book is borrowed from a lyric in the anti-apartheid protest song "Weeping" by Dan Heymann, Ian Cohen, Peter Cohen, and Tom Fox of the band Bright Blue. The story in this book is my attempt to listen to the soundtrack of my childhood and interpret a language in which roaring and weeping share the same father.

This story is not a movie. It is not fiction. And in places it may be as painful for you to read as it was for me and others to live. I like to watch movie trailers because I want to be prepared for the plot I'm about to step into. This one includes emotional, verbal, physical, and racial violence. I want you to be prepared, and I'm grateful if you choose to keep reading. Because that isn't the end of the story. There is hope ahead.

It Wasn't Roaring, It Was Weeping

My Fatherland

My father is my native land. The map of all my own
rift valleys, mountain peaks, and wildernesses. He smells like
sharp cologne and soft leather in the mornings, sweet Old
Brown Sherry in the evenings, and the antiseptic cleanliness of
a doctor who has been scrubbing his hands for six decades. He
has lived all his days under South African skies except for the
three winters of snow chains and shocked frozen windshields
when he was a grad student at seminary in Philadelphia. How
could he and I have known that like the huff and puff of a
dandelion, the seeds of those American years would blow into
our future? That after growing up like the lyric of a Paul Simon
song, with "mission music . . . ringing 'round my nursery
door" in Zululand, South Africa, I would transplant back to
the American East Coast in my own student days? We couldn't
have known that I would accidentally retrace the violent outlines of my father's topography and finally interpret all the
unspoken things between us.

I can picture him. I run my mind like fingers over braille,
reading the memories. He is sitting at the desk in his consult-

ing rooms on the tenth floor of the Louis Pasteur Hospital building in downtown Pretoria. He is wearing a striped dress shirt and tie. The shirt is sometimes white, sometimes blue, sometimes maroon. There might be an ink stain in the breast pocket from his favorite fountain pen that bleeds as often as his patients. His slacks are ironed with a careful crease, and his black leather shoes have been shined and shined again to stretch every last mile out of them. Their soles are scuffed with decades' worth of climbing those ten flights of stairs from the parking lot to the front desk, to squeeze exercise into the beginning of another marathon day of seeing generations of patients over a lifetime of faces.

His back is to the window, where the soundtrack of city life pushes through the cracks in the blinds: a chorus of taxis with their aggressive horns, hawkers at stoplights trying to wheedle you into a new cellphone case before the light turns green, and the joyful bass beat of Kwela music thrumming beneath it all. His desk houses prescription pads and sticky notes and enough pens and colorful markers to have been my favorite place as a child to play pretend secretary or bank manager or doctor.

His hands are the tools of his trade—long, lean fingers with scrupulously clean nails. I have watched those fingers tie off stitches in my shin, pull a six-inch pick-up-stick out of my foot where it was lodged between the knuckle bones of my big toe, swab the long cut on my firstborn's ankle, and once, while I held the surgical thread, stitch up a jagged cut in his left hand with his right. He has a doctor's hands. And, like the rest of him, the skin on those hands has surprised me by aging. It is soft now, like glossy parchment paper, evidence of surprising mortality. Those hands are a map of veins as blue as the South

African sky, pockmarked by a Southern-Cross galaxy of age spots and freckles and faith after years of folding them in prayer.

He is the larger-than-life character who ruled the kingdom of my childhood, the hero or the villain, depending on the day's plotline.

And his voice trembles in my ear this morning.

I press the phone tight to my head so that nothing is lost in translation in this conversation taking place across time zones and oceans. It's a Wednesday afternoon in Maryland and I am not sad today. I tell myself I am not sad that this is the date my mother died. Because it is also the date when years later I discovered I was pregnant with our youngest child, a daughter. She is thirteen now and her name in Greek means "life." I am not sad, because thirty-two years is a very long time and I have sung the anthem of grief on repeat for years, and today I am able to hear it without a catch in my throat. It has become part of the backdrop of my story and no longer the protagonist.

But my dad is crying. In his voice I hear the treble of home; we are a country of twelve national languages. On his tongue I catch the British English of his ancestors and the guttural Dutch Afrikaans of his childhood on the farm. My father speaks three or four languages, depending on how strictly you define "speaks," and he can enunciate the elusive clicks of isiXhosa, but isiZulu is what he shrugs on when he is going for quick connection because it's where he's most comfortable. He speaks in the language he happens to be thinking in, and it still fascinates me to listen to him switch back and forth without pausing to reorient his tongue.

I am sitting in a nest of early fall blankets on my bed in Maryland, but I am now also standing in the South African spring sunshine across from my father's desk, listening to him and hearing echoes of the deep timbre of a Zulu choir, the harsh bark of the hyena, the ululation of joy, of grief, the cry of a beloved country that carries the shame of the most institutionally racist scars since Nazi Germany. That is a lot to crowd into a small room. But my dad is South Africa personified to me. And in my mind, I sit down across from him and lean in to hear what language he's speaking today.

Turns out it is the language of regret, and it sounds the same in any tongue. It is native to me as a South African. And also as a motherless daughter.

"The thing is," he says in a strained, quiet voice, "your mom got the worst years of my life."

And there it is.

At seventy-seven he can't go back and unmake his story. His confession is surprising in its honesty and also its accuracy. I realize he is not crying for himself. He is crying for my mom, the wife of his youth. He is crying the lament of the too late. That terrible song that gets stuck on repeat in our heads in the midnight hour. That haunts us when we look back at the baby pictures and see reminders of every single time we lost our temper and yelled bloody murder when, drained of every emotional reserve, our fifteen minutes alone got interrupted, again, by someone who couldn't find their shoes and treated us like a human search engine instead of figuring it out themselves.

Or maybe it's the regret of the mundane: the rental house you still haven't moved out of, the debts you still haven't paid off, the grocery list of daily disappointments that are choking you.

Then there are the twists and turns in a storyline that went completely off script. We were promised one thing and instead, like grown-up children expecting delight and awe, we got coal, over and over and over again. Until our stockings are stuffed so full of disappointment we ache for a refund, a do-over, a ban on all movies with perky, perfect families and parents who say just the right thing at just the right time. We wake up on Saturday mornings and no one is bringing us coffee in bed or racing out to pick up pastries before kissing our necks, the dip and curve of our hips. Instead, we are in counseling while still waking up next to the person with morning breath and irritating habits and grudges that spoon us. The banal reality is that we come from human homes where messing up and trying again is our daily bread.

And then there are the real scars that cut much deeper than irritation or tired parenting or the job that hasn't brought joy in years. There are the choices that are deliberate, cruel, and if you close your eyes right now you can remember how they felt—whether you were on the giving or receiving end. I remember mine. I remember growing up like a teenage munitions expert who traveled unpredictable roads, never sure when her foot would hit an IED planted by my father. I could usually defuse his temper with my eyes closed. I could pick up on the slightest vibration in the air, the tremble in the atmosphere as the house held its breath on the nights my father came home tired and stressed. And in the years after my mom died this became my full-time occupation: trying to predict the signs before an explosion. I never could quite pin it down. Our house had holes in the walls. I don't mean metaphorically.

I sit in my bed in Maryland, and I listen to my dad, and I think about a kind of ocean deeper than the Atlantic. An ocean so many of us drown in because we can't keep treading water in a sea of daily regret. I think about the last three years that have been the hardest in my marriage and the twenty-two before that.

I think about all the things I've messed up, and I hear my dad speak again: "It's like you grew up the child of an alcoholic." Except his drink of choice was rage; his addiction, righteous indignation.

His voice is crumpling, and we are far out to sea now in a tiny dinghy with two oars and a howling gale, hugging the small boat.

"I look at my younger kids now," he says, "and I think, *It's not fair. It's not fair you didn't get to have this kind of dad.*"

I have a second mother now, close as a sister, who has forever laid to rest the ghost of Cinderella's stepmother. Along with her own two kids, together she and my dad have given us four adopted siblings. And it's like this second generation is being raised by a completely different parent than the one who sired my brothers and me.

"And it's too late. I can't change anything," he's saying. "I can't go back and give you the dad you deserved. I can't give her the husband I am now."

His hazel eyes are full of all the things he would have done differently, and I can hear the urgency in his voice, the sense of time running through his fingers like sand spilled out of a broken hourglass. I feel it too. My kids are teens now and my summers with them still at home are running out and there is a knot in my stomach because what if I'm too late like my dad?

I lean my head against the phone, like I wish I could lean it against his shoulder. He is my longitude and latitude. I inherited his height and temper and, now, also his regret. People always tell me I have my father's smile. In every photograph, it is crooked on one side like my mother's, but it is shaped as if someone had traced over my dad's grin and photoshopped it onto my face. We smile the same and we weep the same.

"But, Dad," I hear myself say, "that's not the whole story."

I feel a resistance in my gut. Something is pushing back against his ending to our story.

He is seventy-seven. I am fifty. I don't know what age you are. I don't know if you left when you should have stayed, hated when you should have forgiven, broke trust when you should have been faithful. But I do know what it feels like to believe you're too late. That there's been too much damage. That the only way forward is repeating where you came from. That you're too angry, too sad, too far gone for a rewrite. I know that very, very well. I hear it in my dad's voice and my worst three-A.M. fears. I read it in the history of my motherland, South Africa, and the headlines of my adopted homeland, America. Regret is both individual and universal, personal and communal.

And still.

And still, that is not the whole story.

I want to tell you the whole story. Or at least, a more whole story.

I want to unpick the plot points that were impossible to make sense of while we were living them and explain to you why you're not too late. That some stories don't have to be repeated. That new stories are waiting to be written in your bloodline.

But you'll have to trust me.

I'm in a Dunkin' Donuts drive-through when I send that message to my dad. "You're going to have to trust me," I tell him. "I'm going to write our story. I'm going to tell the story of you and me and South Africa. Because if it wasn't too late for us, then it's not too late for anyone."

I disconnect. I drink my coffee. I go to work. I go to bed.

I wake up the next morning and there it is, the message from him, blinking on my phone. I'm not ready to listen to it yet. I save it until later in the afternoon. And then suddenly I have to hear it right away. I can't sit still and listen. I get up. I go outside. I walk down the driveway. I look up at the ancient oak trees that have been bearing witness for generations. I listen. And his accent comes through in his British South African English, and he says what I hoped he would: "My darling. Write our story. Write whatever you need to; I don't know what could possibly be worth sharing about my life. But, if it will help one person, tell our story."

So, I am going to.

CHAPTER 1

Family Thorn Tree

I remember the exact moment when I knew I'd become my father.

The memory isn't a visual one. It's a visceral one. I don't remember the moment like you remember a story. I remember the moment like you feel an emotion. Like seeing an old photo that falls out of a book and you can't remember what happened the day the photo was taken. You don't remember what time it was or what season or what any of you were eating, drinking, or talking about. You recognize your dining room table and your middle son and the blurry faces of your two other children, but you can't describe what came before or what came after the photograph.

All there is is the snapshot. Suspended in time. It stands alone.

But the emotion roars in my memory.

It was an out-of-body experience.

The only other times I have felt that kind of adrenaline-pumping, sweaty, jaw-clenching aching of bunched muscles laying siege to the body that shakes with the tremors of its own internal earthquake pushing up, up, up, from the lower intestines through the straining tendons in the neck, forearms, and fists and out the vocal cords, vibrating with the falsetto of rage, was when it was directed at me. When it was my father's body, his tendons, his voice.

But this wasn't my father now, here. It was my own body clenched with the oncoming tsunami of rage. I felt the explosion like a kind of beautiful blackout. Like suddenly all the patience and exhausted reasonableness that I'd been holding on to, that had been slipping like a fraying wire through my hands, finally snapped, and as the metal sliced through my palms and I unclenched my fingers and gave up the battle to hold on to my reason and my polite voice, all I felt was relief.

The tension in my shoulders, the fear in my belly, the despair in my heart after hours of hostage-negotiation-level parenting were erased by a single blissful feeling. A pure, unadulterated orgy of anger swept all other parenting feelings and failings aside like they were nothing, like they were tiny twigs drowned beneath Niagara Falls.

And I bore down in my anger, like the day I delivered him into the world, and placed my forehead level with my middle son's head and let my eyes burn into his ten-year-old reflection of me. And I opened my mouth and let the freight train come screaming out.

I don't remember what I said. I only know that I screamed so loud and so long that for days afterward my voice was hoarse and my throat ached like an overused muscle. I punctuated my screams, my sarcasm, my venom with my hands slamming down on the table. The beautiful, broad beams of a pine table that I'd stained rich, dark chocolate shook under my hands. Scream, slap the table, roar, slam the planks, gasp down air, scream again. I pounded my point home.

Like I said, it was an out-of-body experience.

I watched him watching me. His mother. This wasn't our first rodeo. He knew what was coming. I watched him brace. I watched him holding in all his fear, his confusion, his despair in his tight-pinched mouth and burning cheeks, willing himself not to let his own wail out. I watched myself terrorize my son. I watched his spirit cower behind his eyes, behind the tears he was too embarrassed to let fall, watching me and waiting for it to be over. Trying to become as small and still as possible so as not to step on another landmine. I watched and I recognized the signs of my own terrified childhood. And still I kept screaming. I *chose* to keep screaming.

And as I hovered outside myself, watching the lava pour out of my mouth, one single thought shot ice-cold through my inferno: *I am my father.*

* * *

I have often thought my father would have made an excellent Napoleon or Admiral Nelson. He is a man wired for conflict, for battle, who isn't suited to the domestic niceties of small talk or political correctness. I could have seen him driving an ox wagon and staking his claim on the fertile farmland and freedom that the *Voortrekkers,* literally translated "front pullers" in Afrikaans—South Africa's version of pioneers—came in search of. I could have seen him commanding a ship, mapping out new trade routes, leading mighty men into battle. He is a man wired for action, as hard on himself as those around him.

And my imagination is tamer than the truth. My father's side of the family tree has wild branches that grew right out of an H. Rider Haggard novel. He has an ancestor who was an admiral in the British Royal Navy, served during the Napoleonic Wars, and was later a member of Parliament and a leading figure in British horse racing. He was the second son of the 1st Earl of Stradbroke. He joined the navy at thirteen. His older brother joined the army at sixteen and earned the Military General Service Medal, reached the rank of captain, and was injured during Wellington's campaign and so missed out on Napoleon's defeat at the Battle of Waterloo by just two days. Battles are in my bloodlines. And my veins.

This family tree grows wild, knobby, and knotty, between the first and second floors of my father's house in South Africa. A forest of births and marriages and deaths, names and layers of history that my dad researched and tended on his wall, marking the sepia photos with tiny Letraset numbers to match the faces to the names. Like living bark pressed between the glass photo panes. Entering the house was to walk under their shadow. Their frozen faces watched our comings and goings, the past silently bearing witness to the battles still raging in the present.

When I was a child, I thought like a child. I thought those people on the wall had very little to do with the nine hours we used to drive every summer holiday from our home in Pretoria, capital city of South Africa, to the middle-of-nowhere, one-traffic-light town of Middelburg, a small hamlet stranded in the Karoo, the vast interior of the country—a region the size of New Mexico with scrubby desert as far as the eye can see. The Khoikhoi people were the first to walk its dirt and call it *Karoo,* meaning "hard, dry; a land without water." The

Karoo is our outback, and Middelburg literally translated means "Middle Town" because of its location—a wilderness pit stop halfway between the twin metropolises of Pretoria and Cape Town. It also marked the location on the map of my childhood of every memory that grew out of my father's family tree. Because thirty minutes outside of Middelburg was the sheep farm where my father grew up, named after his British ancestor, the Earl of Stradbroke, and his warring sons.

To my child's eye, the name was as nondescript as any other street sign, the green reflective background and the white letters simply spelling out the turnoff for our farm. It was a name I accepted at face value, never making the connection to the photos on our wall back home. Stradbroke was simply the odd name of a farm on a sign on the long strip of highway outside a town in the middle of nowhere. It was the marker that told us we'd reached the end of a journey that felt endless to a child. At the sign, my brothers and I would sit up, roll down the windows, and breathe in the dry dirt road that turned off the highway and ran like a vein into the South African escarpment, offering adrenaline, adventure, and playing at farming. I didn't realize it was a living thing, that name. I still thought like a child.

How could I know at ten that the scream echoing around my dining room table in Hanover, Maryland, at forty-four would have its origin on that farm, grown from that family thorn tree? But we are none of us lone rangers; every dandelion seed, no matter how far it was huffed and puffed from its origin story, carries the chloroplast DNA of its ancestors. Scientists can trace how plant populations move by studying their seed dispersal. What grew in Maryland blew across the Atlantic from the Karoo and before that must have swirled and seethed across the seas on board an admiral's vessel that, once upon a time, set sail from England and docked at the Cape of Good Hope.

* * *

My dad and I go horseback riding on Stradbroke. I am in the fourth grade. I am as intimidated by my horse as I am in love with her. She isn't really mine. She is a workhorse here on the farm. But when we are visiting, she is mine. Her name is Sherry, her mane and coat soaked with the rich colors of her name. We ride out early while it is still cool, before the sun can burn your neck the bright pink of a city girl out of place on a farm. My dad rides the stallion who immediately understands there is another alpha on this outing.

The horses dance and skitter down the crunchy driveway behind the kitchen, where the feral cats have all been called to breakfast by the maids. I follow my father along the well-worn route of his childhood, the driveway sweeping around the house, from the tack room and horse corrals in the back, where the cats are now crowded around the massive metal saucers of leftover milk and cream from the morning's milking, to the lush green gardens in the front. The British colonial style house has no air-conditioning, but the bedrooms that line the right-hand wing all have doors opening directly onto the colonnaded veranda that runs alongside the house, with its oxblood tiles and steps down to the driveway, easy-always access to the work of farming that calls to you night and day.

My skinny butt bumps in the saddle and anticipates the ache that will arrive by this afternoon, the stiffness of a tourist. My inner thighs chafe against the stirrup leathers, and my riding school jodhpurs will get a workout today like they aren't used to. This is no one-hour class, no polite instructor, no safe layer of sawdust to catch you if you fall.

The horses huff out against the morning air and, in the distance, I can hear the cattle that have been milked, calling to their calves, the buckets now full on their way to the dairy to be poured through an old hand-crank separator, parsing the milk from the cream. There is the clanging of pails and the generator and the windmill up on the hill behind the house groaning its weary, metallic cry as it winds wind into power. My father has shape-shifted from city doctor to third-generation farmer. I see it in his muscle memory as he sits, long legs straddling the western-style saddle, bush hat cocked against the sunrise, left hand resting on the pommel.

We pass the garden with its fishpond and flower beds, fruit trees and pockets of shade splayed out almost indecently in this land of dust, heat, and dun-colored veld as far as the eye can see in every direction. We pass the aloes and reach the perimeter of the house and garden and boundary between what has been tamed and what is still the Great Karoo, calling to that thing in my heart that doesn't yet understand that history isn't just something you study in school. It's trapped inside of you, throbbing beneath your rib cage. My dad sidles his great bay up to the gate and nudges it close enough with his knee that he can loop the top of the fence post out from under the restraining wire, and the big beast pushes his chest, unafraid, into the gate that slowly gives way. I follow and my father repeats the process to close the gate, circling back around and gazing down the long rutted road toward the sheep camps.

This land has its own language—ride out to number 6 camp to check the water troughs, round up the ewes in *Meerkat Vlaktes* Camp, check the baboon trap from the *Draai,* never race a horse down the steep and cobbled Marratta Pass. There is no part of this land that my father doesn't know by sight or smell or memory. He is the youngest child of four by a full decade. A Joseph who grew up with no clue that his father's devotion was as unusual as it was divisive. "Old Blue" they called his dad, my grandfather. Because in his fifties he signed up to go to war, his piercing blue eyes hard and proud as he declared that "No damn Germans" were going to invade his land. He left his partially deaf wife to run his farm and raise his three children as he shipped out with men half his age for North Africa. We have his pith helmet and his stories from Egypt.

It was these wild card volunteers who made South Africa's entry into the Second World War possible because at the time the entire army numbered only about five thousand regulars. Conscription was impossible because on the eve of declaring war in 1939, the country was a twisted pretzel of political and military complications. They went something like this: (a) while South Africa's head of state was legally the British king, (b) its prime minister, J. B. M. Hertzog, was the leader of the anti-British National Party and sympathetic to the Nazi systems of racial segregation, but in a weird twist of fate, (c) to solidify power five years earlier had joined in a unity government with the pro-British South African Party of Jan Smuts.

So, while South Africa was constitutionally obligated to support Great Britain against Nazi Germany, it was only a narrow margin of Parliament that supported that position. Further complicating the realities of war was the fact that South Africa's race policies refused to consider enlisting troops from the majority Black population and would arm only men of European descent. The final twist was that prewar plans never anticipated the fight moving outside southern Africa, and the limited army was trained and equipped only for local bush warfare. Grandpa would bring the remnants of that war back with him, still fighting it in his mind long after his body was home on the farm.

We trot past a field of saltbush, grown here in the Karoo because of its headstrong genetic makeup, its ability to weather drought after drought and still offer our sheep the nutrients they need. They call it "Old Man Saltbush," and when combined with our will-eat-anything South African Dorper sheep, you get lamb with high levels of vitamin E and consumer appeal for the foodie-est of foodies, since the meat's quality and flavor is equal to grain-fed lamb.[1] All I knew back then was that the sheep were survivors. As tough as the people who farmed them. Sherry surprised me once while we were herding a huge flock by bending down and nipping their woolly backsides to encourage the stragglers to keep up. Horses, sheep, farmers, escarpment, and layers of color and complication are all there in the early morning sunrise and our history.

My dad nudges his stallion into a slow lope down the road and I sit, ramrod straight, like I have been taught, elbows perpendicular to my body, and follow his trail of dust puffs. I take big swigs of this big sky air. My hair is in a ponytail that I can feel bouncing against the back of my neck.

My dad is narrating the landscape as we ride. "Watch for potholes, okay?" He shifts in his saddle, flicks his reins lightly. "Remember to watch for meerkat holes. A horse can break a leg if you hit one. Those things will catch you if you're not careful." My eyes scan the veld; I'm doubtful I'll be able to spot one in time to avoid it. But I nod seriously, my saddle making a satisfying leather creak with every shift of Sherry's long limbs.

We jog slowly down the lane. Down by number 4 camp is where my dad once posed with a foot on the hood of his Mercedes-Benz, a long shotgun in his arms. We took picture after picture because he was trying to re-create a photograph of his own grandfather, who once posed like that with his prize stallion and his weapon. I can't remember if that was before or after my mom died. But, years later, my dad would be horrified when he remembered it.

Today we trot by the spot, and he urges me closer, next to him, close enough that if our horses jostle, my knee might bump his. I hold the reins with focus. Right now I am the truest version of myself, invincible on my horse, sweat beading between my shoulder blades and running down my back. On the ground I am too skinny, too tall, too awkward with hair the color of South Africa's rock rabbits, the unattractive but highly durable hyraxes we call *dassies* in Afrikaans. But on horseback, I am this farmer's daughter and the light wind with its slight fragrance of manure seems to sing my name back to me.

To ride out with my dad is to be given an invitation into this hallowed space, where I am a guest in his story. I'm told he got it from my grandfather, but my father is the most vividly gifted storyteller I know. Every evening of my childhood, he sat his three children down around the dining room table, pulled out the Bible, and read and often reenacted before our wide eyes the wild tales from the Old and New Testaments. Part storyteller and part preacher, my dad is the reason it's all but impossible to stump me with even the most obscure Bible references.

Leviticus, Judges, Deuteronomy, bring it. Ecclesiastes, First and Second Samuel, First and Second Kings, I can retell all those stories like they're my own. I have ached for Phalti, second husband of King David's wife Michal, in Second Samuel chapter 3. Bet you didn't know that one, the story where she's dragged back to the once-shepherd-boy-exile, now newly crowned king, away from the man who has loved her in the intervening years, who follows, "weeping behind her all the way" (verse 16).

My father knows Scripture like he knows the history of the Zulu nation. My fire-and-brimstone father quotes Shaka Zulu and his wartime consigliere, Mgobozi, as easily as he does John the Baptist or Paul, the chief of sinners. His is the oral tradition of farmers, of preachers, of Zululand: part folklore, part memory, part Gospel. To ride with him is to ride out into story. So, as we watch for meerkat warrens on behalf of our horses' delicate ankles, I remember the story of the mongoose that was his most beloved pet as a child on this farm. My own children both love and hate that story—how the creature from Meerkat Manor became more faithful than a dog and would follow my father from room to room until the day it accidentally got caught in a slammed door, my dad unaware that the little fella was right on his heels. Or the *rinkhals,* ring-necked spitting cobras he and his best friend from boarding school would catch and sell during the school holidays, shipping them via large tins that had holes poked through the lid from the inside to protect the snakes from injury. Wrapped up in brown paper packages tied up with string and a label that said, "Beware live snake." And the day Grandma came into his room and was bending over making a bed when she felt the wet violence, shot through the cage she didn't know was hidden behind her, dripping down the back of her knees. Or the goshawk that he stalked high up into the topmost stories of a eucalyptus tree to try to poach a chick from the clutch, risking the outraged kamikaze swoop of the four-foot wingspan and grizzled beak of the screaming female raptor.

His father had hired a young best friend from one of the staff families to keep his son company on these escapades. My dad didn't know about the deal. He tells me years later how he always wondered if his best friendship was a two-way street or simply a transaction. My grandpa, like all veterans, had come home from the war changed. But without the language to interpret trauma back then, his oddities were simply accepted as the divine right of the *"Groot Baas"*—the big boss. He'd roar around the farm at night in his pickup truck, lights blazing, horn blaring, an act of defiance in the mind of a man who'd spent four years silently picking his way across the deserts of North Africa.

My grandma had ruled in his absence, a lone woman stranded miles away from Middelburg, surrounded by the vast sea of some of the harshest farming territory, running the family sheep farm with an iron fist and a pristine tea service every morning and afternoon. She'd been hard of hearing before my father was born. But when Grandpa came home and they produced their post-war baby, the doctor told her that the pregnancy would cost her her hearing altogether; he recommended termination.

She refused. And as she pushed my father into the world, her sense of hearing was pushed out completely.

But her husband would find his equilibrium again, and the man who, in his own words, "grew up with curses, cuffs, and kicks" would fall in love with the boy he would give his name and one day his farm.

So, when we ride out, I swell with the feeling of the first-born heir. What I don't know is that we will lose all this. Cancer will take my mother, and the hospital bills will take our farm. And there are stories of weeping that have watered this red soil, but I don't know those today. Today, I am my father's daughter, and this fills me with pride.

We reach the base of the small hill called *Vaalkop,* which means "pale head" in Afrikaans. With its base of shifting shale and hard, pale rock caking the top of the rise, it is nature's own half-pipe that we race up from the level floor of the veld, gaining speed, and thrill as we chase each other up onto the raised dome, a living, breathing game of "King of the Castle."

I hear my dad flick his reins, and over his shoulder he says, "Let's go!" I gulp in air and grab a handful of mane to brace myself as Sherry anticipates the shift in our rhythm, and the gallop explodes under me. The scrubby land flashes by below me and I'm trying to watch for meerkat and *dassie* holes, suitably afraid of the danger that those natural landmines can spell for a horse. But it's impossible. The earth is a sweaty blur of red rocks, golden grasses, and gray-green bushes. The occasional acacia tree reaches out a spiked and twisted finger, long thorns that will whip your cheeks and arms with welts that water red. My father is all elbows and long legs, whooping and hollering as the stallion flies, neck stretched out, wild as the land beneath them. We are an anthem then and it's beautiful, the thunder of hooves, the rush of veld and wind, and the joy pounding out of me with every hard breath. I'm laughing and whooping along with my dad.

We come down slowly from the high and turn the horses' noses in the direction of home. The air is alive around us, the sharp cry of a black eagle circling so far above us, it's a speck I can barely see; the wind that has its own strange quality, singing down from the mountain, cool and fresh and coating my nostrils with dust; and the rhythmic crunch of horse hooves on gravel and brush. My heart is a hot buttered biscuit, filling the rest of me with the satisfaction of being in a place where you are known in a way that mountains are known—for their permanence. This place can trace my people back for generations.

In the last mile before home there is a long camp that we have to cross before we meet up with the road again. It beckons us to race. I am ready for another chorus, and we take off, a humming hymn of joy. Until I realize my dad's bass beat isn't delighted like mine is anymore. No. His is furious.

He is furious with his horse, who is jacked up on adrenaline and ignoring the commands coming its way. I catch my dad's voice on the wind: "Stop it! Stop your bloody nonsense!"

The stallion's nostrils flare red; he is now trotting, now cantering, in sharp staccato steps along a diagonal, his proud neck refusing to submit. The two are locked in a battle of wills.

My dad is using his reins like a whip, slapping the stallion's neck, back and forth, back and forth, the leathers flying as he curses the animal for its violence. "Damn you. Damn you! Stay. Stand still. Listen to me, dammit! You bloody better listen."

The horse dances wildly, metabolizing the rage pouring off my father. Until my dad makes a fist and punches the horse in the neck.

"*Jou Bliksem!* You devil! Damn you, behave!"

And my eyes grow wide along with the horse's, and we are both of us unsure of ourselves. I slow beside my father, keeping my distance and my silence. Meerkat holes become irrelevant. I do what I always do. I project quiet. I hold in my face and my feelings. I simply let the rage roll over me like a tidal wave, and I duck dive beneath it, coming up with as little spray getting into my lungs as possible. I keep breathing. I ride to the side of my father, but behind him. We are almost at a walk now.

Until he notices, and it infuriates him. "What are you doing? Are you some kind of bloody servant now, riding behind me?"

He gesticulates for me to come alongside him and the stallion that is now prancing sideways in its own violent confusion. I get closer to the gravitational pull of this man who is my story. And I wait. Like lighter fluid spilled on a fire, I know the blaze will be bright and scary and just as quickly will burn out. When it does, I know it will be okay to speak. I always know what to say. As his fire burns out, I tell my father, "Wow, Dad, the farm is just gorgeous today."

He swats at a horsefly. Looks up. Adjusts his hat and his seat in the saddle. Looks over at me. And right there, in the updraft of sparks still smoldering from the burn, he grins at me. "Yes, whew, yes, it's magic, isn't it?"

We keep riding. And it's true. This land is a kind of deep and powerful magic.

CHAPTER 2

Tea and Baboons

When we swing our horses toward home, the farm stretches out before us like a fairy tale. Thousands of acres the color of the yellowwood floorboards of a Cape Dutch house roll out from the foot of our mesa mountain shaped like a table. We call it *Tafelberg* in Afrikaans, Table Mountain in English, like its namesake, the more famous tourist destination mountain in Cape Town. Shaped like a tabletop grand enough for the house of a giant or a god, the mountain is a landmark of our farm and this stretch of the Eastern Cape. Aside from its mighty silhouette against the sky, the land is flat as far as the eye can see. And in the distance a thin finger of road runs through the only other visible mountain range, marking the southern border of our farm before it dips down into Cradock, Bedford, Grahamstown, and the coast beyond.

Occasional rich fields of green lucerne shock against the vast dryness, and we trot slowly down around the *Draai*. Afrikaans for "turn," it's the bend in the road leading either away from or back toward the farmhouse. We point our horses' noses toward the house, and I feel Sherry's muscles bunching beneath my scrawny frame.

"Watch her now. Watch! Don't let her get her head." My dad has growled this warning every single time we have ever turned for home with horses who know the way better than we do. I know that if I give even the slightest bit of rein, let go my focused knees for even a moment, my farm-smart horse will snatch the bit out of my hands and charge for home. This is the sport of the men who usually ride them. I am a girl with soft hands and a hard father who will not stomach disobedience from human or equine. My palms chafe as the reins fight me, as I fight my horse. The leather is sweaty and slipping through my fingers, and I clamp my fists exactly as I shouldn't, wrapping the straps as tight around my palms as I can, tethering myself to half a ton of horseflesh that will surely drag me behind her if I come off, but communicating, "Slow, slow, this is where we go slow" with my whole body that sinks into the horse and leans backward.

It's hard to resist the temptation of speed. A galloping horse is the closest thing to flying for the earthbound. Our mounts are dancing now, the two-step of the impatient, the thirsty, the proud. I can tell my father is itching too. He looks over at me. "Can you handle a canter?"

"Yes," I say. I can't imagine saying any other word to my father. My heart jumps like a *springhaas,* the springhares we hunt at night from the back of a pickup truck, ducking after them, tracking them by mounted spotlight, racing them into the veld to try to snag a hind leg by hand. I bunch up my muscles, swipe each sweaty palm, one and then the other, down my jodhpur leg, and take a fresh grip on the reins. I bite the inside of my cheek and then remember I don't want to accidentally bite my own tongue. And then there isn't time for thinking anymore because the horses realize they have won the war and we are flying.

The sun is fully awake now, and the sky is the lightest blue crayon from a coloring box. Sherry chases her sire, and I am along for the ride. To the right is open farmland. To the left is a low tumbledown hillside and beyond it the dam and windmill and willow trees sunk deep into the mud and stranded in a vast lake of cracked dust when the waters recede in the drought seasons. Up ahead on the left are the milking *kraals,* or pens, and the dairy and the small whitewashed chapel that used to be a staff house. And before them, as we hit the rough bits of road pockmarked with cobblestones and broken shards of tile or bits of glass bottles, we slow ever so slightly, and the staff houses come into view. They are tiny postage stamps against the hillside, a row of one- and two-room silhouettes supposed to be the civilized version of Ciskei huts.

Power poles stretch up much taller than the homes and power lines like stitches across the sky knit the tiny patches of white together. They are like something a child might draw, square boxes with rectangular window eyes. People are outside getting water from the taps mounted by their front doors, a parting gift from my grandpa before he died—running water and power. But there are no toilets, and as I race past, I can smell the pit latrines on the wind hitting my face. Children come running at the sound of our pounding hooves, and I want to wave but it's risky to let go one of my reins. I hear them calling my name on the air: *"Nonnie! Haai daar!* Hi there, *Nonnie!"* Waving then giving chase, knees pumping under cut-off school shorts and sock-less sneakers, running alongside our trail with wide smiles.

I cross my left rein into my right hand as the drum of the canter jars through me and fling an arm up to wave, a giant smile on my pink face, my Afrikaans title ringing in my ears. From the first time I arrived on this farm as a baby pushed around in a giant blue perambulator and a lacy white bonnet till my last as a senior in high school when we buried my mother at the foot of the hills in Meerkatvlaktes (Meerkat Plains), I would be addressed as such, *"Nonnie."* You can look it up in the dictionary of South African English, where it is translated as "A respectful term of address or reference used often by [Black] servants to a young unmarried [White] woman or to a [White] girl, often the daughter of the employer."[1] But I don't ever look it up. I know what it means. It means I am special and important and I never, not once, consider a deeper meaning.

I know nothing about the children waving to me other than that to wave back brings me joy. So I assume that a shared joyful existence is mutual. I don't know that they are from the Xhosa tribe. I don't know that they've picked up Afrikaans as part of their parents' migration from the Ciskei, the "homeland" area where our government has forcibly relocated their people, this side of the mighty Kei River. I don't know that this adopted language is evidence of their family's search for work from Afrikaans-speaking farmers. I don't know the origin story behind the blankets the women wear pinned with large safety pins around their waists, or tied around their chests, strapping babies to their backs. I don't know that the Xhosa are often called the "Red Blanket People."

The boy my age with the red T-shirt, faded from a hand-me-down life so that it's now just a dirty orange, fraying in the shoulders, flashes by. I don't question my name and I don't question how our staff live. I just know it is not how we live. Their homes are a background detail in the painting of my favorite holiday scene. Interesting local texture, a curiosity, these people who I don't think about enough to wonder why a whole family would ever choose to live in a one-room dwelling with no indoor plumbing, the size of my farmhouse bedroom. If my mind's eye ever wanders to that part of the painting at all, it's simply a flickering glance, presuming this way of life is cultural preference. While I speak it, I do not yet understand the language of cultural oppression.

* * *

The mothers of those children are waiting to serve us tea when we get back from our ride. Tea is a sacred ritual to my father's people, the British. You can set your clock by it. Served every morning at eleven and every afternoon at four by my grandmother while she was still on the farm and then, when my grandfather died and she'd retired to town, by our farm manager's wife. And nowadays I'm the one boiling the hot water, buying the Five Roses or Rooibos teabags from home, via Amazon, and pouring cold milk into the teacups before pouring in the dark stream of scalding comfort because I was taught the cool milk prevents the delicate china cups from cracking.

If ritual is an act done on repeat and ceremony is a ritual with a religious purpose, then teatime on the farm was church. It was always served at the long farmhouse table in the dining room, with its dark green walls and doors opening onto the sunroom. And sometimes, on special occasions, under the giant thorn tree in the rose garden. My grandmother's tea service was Blue Italian Spode, a design with as much lore and literature behind it as an Italian film star. Launched by the Spode company in 1816, it was an English brand of pottery and homeware that featured a blue and white painted scene inspired by the Italian countryside, combined with a "finely detailed eighteenth-century Imari Oriental border."[2] My grandma was a stickler for table manners. I knew not to put my elbows on the table, to remove my starched and ironed napkin from the heavy silver napkin holder and place it on my lap, and to use the delicate tongs to neatly drop cubes of sugar into my cup.

Most of the Blue Italian Spode pieces produced in the early 1800s were designed with the wealthy in mind—"asparagus servers, huge meat dishes, enormous soup tureens with ladles, cruet sets, foot baths, and more. Many a graceful home used *Spode's Italian*."[3] Against the backdrop of war, drought, and backbreaking work, my father's family aspired to be a graceful home. Like a poor man's *Downton Abbey,* Stradbroke was the manor without the massive fortune, still loath to let down its namesake, and so the tea bell was literally rung twice a day.

When my father was my age, he remembers Mina, the tall Xhosa maid of his childhood, standing patiently during every dinner course, her back to the wall, wearing cap, uniform, and apron and, on special occasions when the family was entertaining guests, a pair of small white gloves. She always served the dishes, as his mother insisted was the proper etiquette, from the left-hand side and cleared from the right.

To this day I can still hear Grandma in my head as I lecture my own kids about how to properly place their knife and fork together to indicate that they're done with their meal—side by side on the right side of the plate in the four o'clock position, with the fork on the inside, tines down, and the knife on the outside, blade in. She would wipe her mouth with a napkin in between bites of mutton and mint sauce and crispy, golden brown roast potatoes and look down the table through her thick glasses and address us fidgety kids: "Now, listen, I know you think I'm just a silly old lady, but learning table manners means you can fit in anywhere you go in the world." I'd work really hard not to roll my eyeballs back in my head. And instead slowly rotate my knife and fork into the approved position, signaling that I was done. She'd watch me like a rock kestrel perched at the head of the table and nod as the maids cleared my plate.

In the scorching heat of summer and the bitter bite of winter, tea was served religiously. Grandpa and his sons—and later Mick, our farm manager, and his sons—would part ways with "the men," the Xhosa male staff, wash up with the green bars of Sunlight soap in the bathroom by the back door, and come stomping in for tea.

After our ride my dad and I follow in their footsteps. My legs are stiff and my hands are coated in that unique mixture of sweat and leather residue from the reins. I stand at the porcelain sink shaped like a cockle shell in the small bathroom off the back hall and watch the ride rinse down the drain. I dry my hands on the soft towels hanging on the water heater; they're worn and warm to the touch.

I can hear the china clinking, and as I make my way down the hall, the floor groans under my feet, the satisfying sound of creaking beams beneath the faded Oriental rugs that are much older than I. The dining room is the gravitational pull at the center of the house, doors opening into it from each of the four walls. The brass doorknobs, the deep mahogany table reflecting the morning light, the gleaming silverware and Sheraton-style sideboard are right out of the set of an *Out of Africa*–style movie before such a thing even existed. You could always smell the furniture wax and leather, and the rooms were an interplay of stingingly bright Karoo sunshine pooling on the cool dark surfaces of the interior.

I pull my chair back from the center of the left-hand side of the long table. Grandma isn't on the farm anymore, but I can still feel her watching me. Uncle Mick sits at the head of the table and his wife, Auntie Christine, sits to his left, and just a few seats up from me is my mom. As is the custom of my people, we call all the adults in our lives by the honorific Aunt and Uncle, whether we are related to them or not. My dad is at the other end of the table, and my brothers and Uncle Mick and Auntie Christine's sons spread around the other seats. My chair is carved from stinkwood; its delicate frame has almost feminine curves, and I plop my tender rear down on the *riempie* seat made of crisscrossing strips of sinewy leather. In the center of the table there are old tin cookie boxes lined with wax paper and full of homemade rusks, the hard biscotti-like biscuits that are made to be dunked into tea, softened, and enjoyed with a cup.

Talk turns to baboons. They are the bane of every farmer we know. My father is stirring his tea in its delicate cup, asking Uncle Mick about the safety of the ewes, and I am picturing him, head thrown back, chest swelling with the inhale, and then throwing his voice with the guttural bark of the massive chacma baboons that plague our farm. My father has the uncanny ability to bark like a baboon. It raises gooseflesh on my arms when he uses it to punctuate his stories. It's a loud, sharp bellow followed immediately by a sharp breath sucked in to form the guttural diphthong of the baboon bark. And it's thrilling to hear my dad throw his baboon call against the cliffs on the farm and listen as it fractures and comes back in a thousand echoes of one of the largest members of the monkey family.

I bite into the soaked end of a rusk, and it crumbles, softened and sweetened by the tea, in my mouth. My arms tingle with the beginning of sunburn and I like how it feels. It means I am not in school, I am not in my routine, I am in this place where the stories are layered and thick like the bold wallpaper around this room. Uncle Mick is updating my dad about the baboon traps.

My dad has walked me into more than one baboon trap to show me how they work. Built from strong beams, they are thick, sturdy cages big enough for several grown men to stand up in. The floor is always littered with the fresh, fat corncobs that we call *mealies*. They are like crack for baboons.

The first time I walked into a baboon trap and my father demonstrated how the trapdoor drops down when a baboon inevitably grabs for the final *mealie* hanging from the trip wire, the hair stood up on my arms. Baboons are the thing of my nightmares. Males can grow to be as big as a man. They have a dark mane on their neck and shoulders. But it's the doglike head with its massive muzzle and heavy brows above beady, close-set eyes that I can picture as I stand in the trap. These alphas have razor-sharp, two-inch-long canine teeth. Standing in that trap with the husks of old *mealies* crunching under my feet, we could see the veld stretching away in all directions, the bleating of sheep a soft sound in the distance.

My dad was crumbling dried kernels off the husks, telling me and my brothers the story behind the traps.

"You know why we have to trap them, yes?" my dad asked.

"Yes," we said, nodding.

"They aren't just predators; they are cruel. In lambing season, they wait for a ewe to drop her lamb and then they tear open her udder to drink the milk." This image will haunt me far into the future.

His eyes narrowed as he glanced up at the horizon, as if we would see the baboons emerging orc-like from the shade of the cliffs.

He adjusted his hat. "They lap up as much milk as they can, eating it right out of the sheep as she lies there dying. And then they just leave." He gesticulated with a furious hand. "They just leave the mother and the lamb to die. They're not interested in them as food. They're just there to feed on the milk and move on. They'll go through as many ewes as they can, ripping and drinking and killing."

He stood, hand on one hip of his dirty blue jeans, thin city belt, blue checkered shirt with long sleeves folded up to the elbows, as he sniffed in, rubbed at his nose, and then yanked on the pulley that opened the straining trapdoor. We were in the *Beeshoek* camp, Cattle Corner in English. It sat across the tar road that divided the farm in two. And after we'd all exited what felt like a giant chicken coop, he demonstrated how the door would slam down once greedy fingers had triggered the spring system baited with *mealies*.

"Baboons will gobble up whatever they find on the floor first. They come in slowly, but when they see all the fresh *mealies*, they realize there's a race to eat the most first." He pointed through the thick chicken wire that covered the whole cage, the dried-up husks evidence of the last time the cage was staged and the trap sprung.

"And then, finally, some smart one realizes there's still one more juicy *mealie* hanging from the top of the cage."

He pointed and our eyes all traveled up to the hook above where we'd been standing a few minutes earlier.

"And when he snatches it . . . boom! The gate slams closed, and we've got him!"

* * *

His patients would be surprised to know how much their civilized big-city doctor knows about baboons. When he was six, my father saw his first baboon fight. My grandpa had got the message, likely from Boesman, the giant Xhosa foreman who used to sometimes heft my young father onto his shoulders, "*Ek dink daar's 'n Bobbejaan daar boe by die Beeshoek lokval. Die deur is toe.* I think there's a baboon up top in the Cattle Corner trap. The trapdoor is down."

And the house sprang into action. Everyone loaded up for the event: my dad's older brothers and sister; his mom; his father; his golden lab, Sandy; and his father's dog, a massive Mastiff Rhodesian Ridgeback named Robert. The result of crossing the native ridged Khoikhoi dog, with its unique hair pattern—a mohawk along the back—and the mastiffs, bloodhounds, Great Danes, and greyhounds brought to Southern Africa by European settlers, Robert and his kind were the original lion hunters. As fast as they are fearless, these dogs weigh in at anywhere from sixty-five to ninety-five pounds. My father was the runt of the pack on this outing.

It's a good twenty- to thirty-minute drive from the farmhouse backtracking to the main gate of Stradbroke, across the strip of tar that is the N10 road to the coast and onto the *Beeshoek* side of the farm. The baboon trap was tucked in close to the mountain range, and as the pickup trucks pulled up, the barking of the baboons was already echoing off the rock face. At least five or six had found themselves trapped and were pawing through what was left of the *mealie* husks, big snouts pausing to sniff the air, push up against the sides of the trap, snap at each other.

There was friction in the air as the pickups unloaded, and electricity snapped between the dogs and the men at the sight and sound of their common enemy. It was loud as the chaos inside and outside the cage bounced off the cliffs and echoed around the quiet veld. Rifles were loaded and cocked, and one by one the boys and men picked off the smaller baboons while the biggest beast barked and snarled from the center of the cage. My grandpa, in his khaki pants and button-down, short-sleeve khaki shirt, whistled for Robert, and the giant dog loped over, quivering with a familiar understanding. Boesman pulled the trap door open, and the dog was a flash of deep auburn, the ridge of hair on its back standing on end, as it shot into the cage.

It was fast. Robert launched himself at the baboon's eighty pounds and a cheer went up. Nipping, diving, driving the big beast in circles, the dog was all jaws and saliva as the baboon whirled from side to side, its white rump flashing, its tail straight up in the air. They sparred and clashed and broke apart, and Robert was yapping and diving back in. But with each turn the baboon's jaw came down again and again on Robert's haunches, his neck, his face until he was whining and pawing the earth.

My father watched Robert, the unbeatable dog, flail as the
baboon's canines closed on his throat. The air was hot and
sticky and thick with howling when Grandma grabbed my
dad's hand and dragged him away from the cage and down
into a dry riverbed screened off from the fight by rows of
scrubby thornbushes. But the barking from baboon and dog
followed them to where they sat on the hot sand.

They waited it out with the robber flies that whirled and
stung their hands, their necks, and they didn't know what was
happening until Grandpa shouted for his wife, "Joan! Joanie,
come quickly!"

And as they stumbled their way over rocks and brush back
to the cage, they saw Grandpa pulling a massive body out of
the cage. My dad assumed it was the carcass of the defeated
baboon. But it was the leonine body of Robert, blood pooling
hot and sticky from the arteries in his neck where the baboon
had torn at his carotid. Boesman was backing up the pickup.
and the boys and men hauled the deadweight of the dog onto
the tailgate and into the bed of the truck as Grandma climbed
in next to him. Trained as a physiotherapist, she pressed her
fingers into the vital pressure point on the great neck, and my
father watched as the blood kept pumping out of that great
heart. She was handed shirts and blankets, and she pushed her
weathered hands down with determined pressure to save the
life that kept dripping into the bed of the pickup.

Boesman would drive them to the vet in Middelburg, and
Grandpa would take the kids home, stunned. Dad doesn't remember how the big baboon died. He only remembers that
Robert lived. It would be weeks before he could come home
though, his great neck shaved and stitches marching like army

ants up and down his neck, his withers, his abdomen. Grandpa would never pit his dog against a baboon again.

* * *

The maids are clearing the tea service, and I am tempted to stick one finger down into my teacup to swipe up the sugar, still warm and sticky at the bottom. I can almost taste its crunch like sweet dirt between my teeth, dissolving on my tongue.

When my parents got married, my mother drank tea from her mother-in-law's Blue Italian Spode at this farmhouse table, and the fine china moved her the way it was supposed to. But my mother, in her innocence or passion or ignorance, casually commented that the blue motif, while beautiful, was "a bit too boring" and was accordingly informed by the matron of the house that if she didn't appreciate it, she certainly wouldn't be inheriting it.

Instead, when my mother set up her own house, she ordered Spode's other bestseller, the Chinese Rose pattern. It was "one of the most popular of Spode's colourful patterns on earthenware in the 20th century."[4] The rich cream background was painted with muted pink, mauve, blue, and maroon flowers in the style of an eighteenth-century Chinese porcelain design. It was a catchy adaptation that appealed to both modern and traditional tastes, as evidenced by my mother's own set and the style's huge success.

When I was the same age my father was when he witnessed his first and last baboon fight, we were living in a neighborhood called Faerie Glen and pouring tea into the Chinese Rose Spode. We were taking tea outside on our recently paved patio at a small white metal table, and I was rocking back and forth in one of the chairs.

"Sit still," my dad barked at me.

I don't think I did. But I can see only the edges of the memory—the tray of dainty Spode teacups and saucers with their delicate, civilized pattern, the rocking chair, my father's voice, the tempting spread.

"I'm telling you, sit still. Sit!"

And too late, the chair met the table, and one tiny cup toppled. The Rose Spode was plucked out of safety and fell, breaking with an almost dainty, tinkling sound.

My father hauled me out of the chair with a roar and then nothing. I can't remember the rest. The details freeze frame right after the breaking cup. There are no other photos in my memory files of that moment. But I think the way the story goes is that he spanked me. And spanked me. And spanked me.

Chapter 3

1984

I thank Auntie Christine for tea. I stand. I carefully push in my chair and wander back to my bedroom with its twin beds and old crocheted blanket, and crouch down, knees already stiffening, in front of the bookshelves, looking for a story I haven't read yet.

I learned to speak books from my mother. The language of literature, poetry, plays, and movie adaptations of the same were her native tongue. An English and Latin teacher, she once told me about a love note a high school student left on her desk. She corrected the spelling and then returned it to him. In our house there was a bookcase built of warm pine stuffed full of all her favorite friends. I'd run my fingers along their spines and say the names of the books out loud and then ask her, "Can I read this one?"

And she'd glance up, consider, and often reply, "You're not ready for that one yet."

"What about this one?"

"You're still a bit too young for that one." And so it would go. Me lingering in front of her history, waiting to be old enough to be let in, each book like a new notch on the growth chart of my mind.

My father was always the oral storyteller, pulling us into the tales with him, revealing his childhood, his dreads, his passions through the telling. My mother was the inhabitant of a more private world that I accessed through the pages of her books. Reading was an act of intentionality for her; books were a map that helped human beings orient themselves in the world.

In tenth grade we were assigned George Orwell's book *1984*, and I was afraid to read it. I'd heard that between its pages lurked rooms where violence was custom-made and torture bespoke, designed to carefully conform to the contours of an individual's unique fears. My mom was sitting in a pool of sunshine on one of our brown corduroy armchairs when I confessed my reluctance to read it.

She put down the book she was reading to look at me through her oversized glasses.

"We'll read it together."

I had thought she'd get me out of reading it.

"We'll read it and discuss each chapter together as you go."

She always believed that to make sense of a story we had to break it down, take it apart, interpret what the writer was trying to communicate. So that you could hear the voice of the author over the voice of his characters. This diluted fear and amplified understanding.

* * *

In 1984, on our farm I drank tea and ate rusks and then read my favorite safari adventure books that had a level of danger and violence a ten-year-old could stomach.

In 1984, our government drank fear and ate its Black and Brown kids for breakfast. In our Orwellian reality of apartheid, racism was codified law, and resistance by thought, word, or deed was violently repressed by the secret police. Twenty thousand people were swallowed up by a national state of emergency over the next two years and held without warrants or charges; almost all were Black, nearly half were schoolchildren, some as young as eleven and twelve. Censorship, the whip, the fist, and electric shock were all used[1] to kill the anti-apartheid momentum. Swearing fealty to his Parliament in the face of possible "punitive measures" from other countries,[2] President P. W. Botha vowed he would not allow the White nation's three-hundred-year heritage "to be placed needlessly on the altar of chaos and decay."[3]

In 1984, in Washington, D.C., President Reagan refused to impose economic sanctions on South Africa, preferring the carrot to the stick. Archbishop Desmond Tutu, who had won the Nobel Peace Prize earlier that year, delivered a speech from Capitol Hill, condemning that choice.[4] And as the state of emergency pulled the noose tighter and tighter around Black necks in South Africa over the next two years, he would plead with the international community, "Only intervention by the outside world can avoid Armageddon. What is the outside world waiting for?"[5]

1984 is a story frozen in time, fossilized on our farm. The Karoo, with its dolerite-capped mountains, ancient time line, and vast semidesert plains, is famous for its fossils. And the footprints of the White Afrikaner tribe, with its fanatical claim as a chosen people, superior race, called by God to take possession of the land and subdue the natives, linger like trace fossils—providing indirect evidence of a past life preserved in the attitudes, anecdotes, and apartness on our farm.

* * *

I wake up on Sunday morning and get dressed for church. My parents have decided to skip the forty-five-minute drive into Middelburg, where the closest Anglican church is gathering with its aunties in hats and farmers struggling into suits. Instead, my dad takes us to join the staff church service. I have no idea if this small gathering is a weekly ritual or for our benefit on the Sundays we happen to be in residence. I am wearing a white cotton blouse with delicate scalloped edges and a lilac skirt with an asymmetrical hemline and pockets. I remember how much I used to love putting my hands in the pockets, pulling the skirt out like a pair of long, low butterfly wings and swaying from side to side. I also have shiny patent leather Mary Janes on my feet, or maybe it's a pair of *tekkies,* the Afrikaans word for sneakers; I can't rightly remember. My mom has tried to get my brothers' hair to cooperate, but it always sticks up straight from their heads.

We head out the back door, past the banked heat of the ancient Aga stove in the kitchen. The maids have already fed the cats and returned home in time for church. We have eaten the breakfast they prepared: bread turned and roasted in the wire toaster on the Aga's boiling plate and served in the silver toast rack. Fresh butter, homemade marmalade, and for my father, the delicacy of sheep's brains on toast, each bite the consistency of a kind of South African cream cheese.

The screen door slams behind us, and I inhale an immediate breath of dust and heat as my father reaches for my hand and my palm is swallowed by his long, sure fingers. He leads us up the path behind the house, through the back gate, up the dirt track littered with bits of broken, weathered glass to the small rise of staff houses. Out in front is the whitewashed building that has been converted into a chapel. I am enchanted. Three steps lead up to the interior, where I duck through the door and adjust my eyes to the dimmer air that is still suffocatingly hot. There are backless wooden benches with staff already seated, wrapped in bright colors, and my brothers and I are shy but sure. I feel welcome here.

My dad preaches but he needs a translator. His isiXhosa is good enough only for a laugh, getting his audience to chuckle at the occasional aside, not for the full Gospel. But I don't remember the sermon; what I remember is the singing. We sing songs in four different languages. This is a place where people don't think in just one language; everything is layered—everyone speaks at least three. Well, everyone Black speaks at least three. Everyone White speaks at least two. Today we sing our way through English, Afrikaans, isiXhosa, and isiZulu choruses. IsiZulu is what I have grown up around. It is the native tongue of the place where I was born. The Xhosa voices slip easily into the isiZulu words; they are rich with the layers of harmony vibrating in the small place, and my heart and hands are the rhythm section. I clap and sway and want to climb inside the music and make it my home. This moment is a memory I carefully fold up like a love letter and tie with a ribbon to tuck into my mind, and no matter where I travel in the world or how old I get, I will be forever bound to the sound of these languages. They are a vibration that imprints on my bones, like the voice of a mother that I am always just on the cusp of understanding.

The service ends long before the singing does. The staff are still clapping and harmonizing as we dance our way out of the chapel, down the steps, and back toward the house. I am sad to leave them. But I take some of their syllables with me, rolling the unfamiliar worship words around in my mouth. And when we get back to the main house, my dad, who has always enjoyed my joy, helps me frame the sounds over and over until we can sing at least one of the songs together. We stand in the hallway, both hands clasped, swaying together as we belt out the isiZulu words, *"Singaba hambayo thina kulomhlaba si-yekhaya, eZulwini.* We may be leaving this world, but we are going home to Heaven." I'd sing it again years later at church camp and the English refrain we sang would go, "I love You, Lord Jesus, 'cause You first loved me, and we're gonna go to heaven for eternity." This moment between us is like a big bubble of glass that has been blown around us, preserving our shared delight inside a snow globe like the ones tourists bring home from the gift store of their favorite foreign destination. And when I look at the globe now, my memories are shaken up and I see how we were tourists inside a Xhosa story.

Back then, there was only one thing that marred my Stradbroke experience. It was the tall blue crane that stalked the property like it owned it. Called by its isiXhosa name, *Indwe,* meaning "Blue Crane," South Africa's national bird. Our *Indwe* had been besotted with my grandfather ever since he rescued it as a chick from the kids who were throwing rocks at it on our neighbor's farm. The young crane had a broken wing by the time Grandpa got to it. He would return daily to feed it water and *mealies* and eventually called our neighbor, who said, "Oh for goodness' sake, yes, please get that crane out of here!"

Grandpa led his love bird home, and while she wouldn't fly

again, she would stalk the property with big eyes surveying the perimeter, watching for her beloved. And when she spotted him, she would launch into a mating dance, calling to Grandpa and extending her neck, undulating her body and hissing at anyone who came close to the pair when they were engaged in the dance.

After Grandpa died, *Indwe* persisted and transferred her affections to my father. The bird was the phantom menace that stalked my twilight evenings, and many a night when I'd be coming in from riding, tired, stiff, and unsuspecting, I'd climb the slate steps onto the wide porch that wrapped around the whole house, heading for the exterior door of my bedroom, the sunset painting the sky cotton candy pink, only to have a bird the size and height of a man explode at me from around a corner in a fit of pique and beak.

My heart would contract as *Indwe* barred my way to the door and hissed her disdain for my size, my gender, my assault on her place and birthright. Wings spread their full six feet, feathers draping all the way to the ground like angry fingers, *Indwe* would flap at me and dance me backward, and I'd retreat, the interloper, small in the face of that kind of preexisting stake. The bird never accepted me. I always dreaded it. And my dad would laugh and dance her attention away from me and my brothers.

* * *

Back in the days when Grandpa still danced with *Indwe,* when fossils were being discovered in the Karoo, when apartheid was being calcified into the DNA of South Africa, my dad and his parents arrived home from town one afternoon to find Mina in the vegetable garden. She was plucking every third or fourth carrot and head of lettuce to tuck into a bundle to be balanced on her head and carried home to her family. And true to their apartheid roots, his parents called the police and had her arrested for stealing. My father watched as tall Mina, bastion of every breakfast, lunch, dinner, and teatime, was loaded up onto the back of the police pickup truck, *bakkie* in Afrikaans, and driven off down the dirt road. The staff watched silently. And my dad stood among them, the people who bathed him, dressed him, played with him, and called him *kleinsir,* little sir, and together they watched the old black-and-white movie reel of cops and robbers play out in real time right before their eyes. Seated in the back of the open van, Mina raised one hand in a wave as she disappeared out of view. My father didn't know if he'd see her again.

And then three days later she was home, and the story picked right back up again. It had been going on for generations. My dad's grandfather had once taken his *sjambok,* the infamous South African leather whips made from hippopotamus or rhinoceros hide, to a young staffer for an offense no one can remember. Because that wasn't the point of the story. The point was that the young man had taken his complaint to the local magistrate, who wrote a letter to my great-grandpa, instructing him to leave off such actions in the future. My dad remembers that the moral of the tale was Great-grandpa's reaction when presented with the letter.

"Ek was by die magistraat. I was at the magistrate." The twentysomething Xhosa faced off with the grizzled White farmer. "He gave me this for you."

And my great-grandpa stood on the back step of the farmhouse, across from the tack room, and looked down at the letter, written in its curling cursive script that he knew the man couldn't read. He looked up, grinned, and replied, *"Ja.* The magistrate says if you give me any trouble, I must beat you again." Which he proceeded to do.

When my dad was fifteen, he watched his own father manage his staff with the same inherited mindset. It was at *tjaile* time, the time of day when the sun dipped low enough that the sticky air could catch its breath. The men were getting ready to knock off and giving final reports to Grandpa when he asked a new staffer, Earnest, who'd been on the farm only about a year, if he'd checked the water troughs up in number 8 camp. Number 8 was the camp farthest from the main house, with a long climb up the rocky *koppie* trail, past the windmill, and over the ridge to make sure the sheep grazing there had what was essential in the dry South African heat.

"Ja, sir! Yes, sir," came back the assurance. So Grandpa waved the men off for the evening and went in to wash up for supper. It wasn't till the next day, when he happened to take the *bakkie* up over the ridge and into number 8 camp, that he found the troughs as dry and cracked as the land around them. The parched flock had come down from their mountain grazing and were milling around, bleating their confusion, rooted to the spot where they should have been able to drink. A full water trough should have lasted for days. It could have been that long again before anyone made the discovery.

My father could feel the rage radiating off his dad as they worked to clean and clear and fill the trough. Water is the Karoo's gold. We drill deep for it. And windmills suck up from the vein that we have struck and fill the reservoir that in turn runs this liquid gold via pipe into the water troughs. A system not unlike what you can see in the back of your toilet's cistern, a small rubber ball floats on top of the water in the trough attached to a valve-like arm that slowly lowers as the water level drops. When the arm sinks low enough, it triggers an automatic refill from the reservoir. Sometimes a frog would get stuck in the pipe or the arm would jam or be knocked off balance by the greedy hooves of thirsty sheep stepping right up and into the trough. Grandpa's anger ran like a live wire through every one of the routine actions to troubleshoot, fix, clean, and refill the trough. A routine day's work that should have been done the day before.

He was as hot and frustrated as his sheep by the time he and my dad got back home, and he slammed into the office in the back of his workshop and yelled at the men to go get Earnest from wherever he was working. No police were called. But when Earnest arrived, his dirty hat slowly removed from his head and literally held in his hands, my dad heard his father say, "Get your stuff, get your family, get everything. You're done on this farm."

"*Wat betekeen jy, sir?* What do you mean, sir?" Earnest asked, confused.

Grandpa barely looked up. "You bloody lied to me about the water in number 8. I just spent all morning cleaning the troughs. You're done on this farm."

It was the heat of the day. Midday under African skies is brutal.

"We're going into town this afternoon. I'll drop you and your family off then."

And under Old Blue's gaze, under the eyes of the ancient hillside and the people who had never told Grandpa or my dad their Xhosa names, a family packed their life up and was loaded onto the back of the pickup and driven down the dirt roads, past the saltbush and lucerne and storybook Table Mountain, and deposited onto the highway a mile or so outside of Middelburg.

"But, Dad," my father said from the front seat, swallowing hard, "but, Dad, there's nothing here."

They were watching as the parents unloaded their three kids and their bundles. The baby started crying, and because there was no shoulder on the highway, which dropped sharply away into a gully peppered with thorn trees, the hastily wrapped packages and bags and bedding slipped and slid and bounced down over the edge of the burning tarmac and into the dusty, thorny embrace below. A life on our farm turned ashes to ashes, dust to dust.

My father was fifteen, and he repeated himself, "Dad, this isn't right. It's too hot. There's no shade. Where will they go?"

There was nothing. There was the black paved strip of tar through the hottest part of the Karoo, a stretch of land so flat that what looked like one mile could just as easily be one hundred. My grandfather was already pulling back onto the road. "Agh, those buggers will be fine. Some other farmer will probably pick them up in less than an hour."

As he pulled away, my father looked back and watched as the mother tried not to trip over her unraveling blanket wrap, holding the screaming baby, trying to avoid the thorns.

Once upon a time my dad had asked Grandpa if Black people were humans like us, created by God. And Grandpa had considered, cocked his bald head, and answered thoughtfully, "I think they're like something in between animals and people."

My dad and my grandfather drove home. In the rearview

mirror, Earnest and his wife tried to save their belongings and their children. My father still couldn't swallow.

*   *   *

"Karoo firewalkers" are what geologists call the dinosaurs that once trekked their way through this semiarid part of the country, leaving their footprints forever fossilized in between volcanic eruptions.[6] They were some of the last animals known to have lived in this inhospitable region before it was swallowed up by molten rock. Middelburg marks the spot in this geological landscape halfway between Pretoria and Cape Town, and then dividing the distance again, halfway between Port Elizabeth and Bloemfontein, and telescoping in even tighter, halfway between Graaff-Reinet and Colesberg. A town caught in the middle of some of South Africa's most fiery eruptions.

The dinosaur of White supremacy had been trekking across the subcontinent since the first dissatisfied Dutch-speaking colonists broke with their Cape community and church in the 1830s in search of a promised land where they would be free from British rule and could establish their own independent land and doctrine. Determined to snuff out all things English and enlightenment, the most conservative sect of this new national religion would call themselves *Doppers*, a bastardized version of the Dutch word *domper*, or "damper" in English—the tool used to extinguish a candle's flame. Their mass migration into the interior of South Africa dragged with it tales of battles that turned rivers red with blood as the new nation cut a covenant with God, as they cut down the Zulu and Xhosa by their tens of thousands. And this sacred folk memory of Afrikaner nationalism climbed out of the veld soaked with the sacrifice of these *Voortrekkers*, brutal pioneers, and into the pages of the first constitution in 1910, which then also proceeded to kill the Black South African's right to vote.

And on September 15, 1914, three hundred delegates of the Cape Province branch of the new National Party would gather in Middelburg, in the land of the firewalkers, and baptize Dr. D. F. Malan as their party's first chairman; the great leviathan grandfather of apartheid, Malan would eventually become prime minister of South Africa. The same town would also spawn Jozua Naudé, who would co-found the Afrikaner *Broederbond* (Brotherhood) in 1918, with an even more fanatical ideological commitment to separatism.[7]

So when my dad and grandfather drove home after depositing Earnest's family on the outskirts of Middelburg, they were driving on the trail of well-preserved history.

Learning to look for tracks, or animal *spoor,* had always been a fun part of our holidays on the farm. I could recognize the *dassie,* the baboon, the droppings of the impala and the kudu. But the only *spoor* of apartheid that I saw when my dad and our family drove that same road twenty years later was the sprawling shantytown of Black families on the outskirts of Middelburg. We always passed it on our way out of town, when we'd taken tea with Grandma and the car was pointed back toward Stradbroke. Our old green Volkswagen station wagon would skim past the rim of another world: corrugated iron roofs, dust where there never were lawns, and giant light poles, their bulbs encased in wrought-iron cages. I would watch that other world flash by me and always wonder why the lights were in cages. Once upon a time my dad explained, "It's to protect the bulbs."

"From what?" I was a stranger in a strange land.

"From stones," he said over his shoulder to the back seat where I was, as usual, battling motion sickness and focusing on the fact that there were only about another forty-five minutes ahead of us before I could stretch and take a deep breath of horses and holiday.

I was still no closer to understanding what he meant. But we were out of the orbit of the township now and I barely registered as he tried to explain one more time, "To stop the kids from shattering the lights; so that the police can keep an eye on the place."

It's a constellation of facts that settles into the back of my mind, like microfossils—those deposits that are an aggregate of their habitat, arrows pointing back to the original environment—waiting for us to unearth them so they can tell their full tale.[8] It will be years before I unearth the full story of Middelburg, South Africa. I will live it, but I won't discover it until I am in law school in South Bend, Indiana, nine thousand miles away, researching a paper on Nelson Mandela. And looking back, I want to pick up shovels, trowels, spades, brushes, sieves, and buckets, the full archaeologist's toolbox, and hammer at the inside of my mind. I don't want to be gentle; I want to excavate my own willful ignorance—terrifying as it emerges—fact by fact, from the sediment inside the deep caves of my mind.

CHAPTER 4

The Slow Kiss Goodbye

When I am twelve, a friend from school joins our family holiday on the farm. I had told her tall tales about stallions and meerkats and the wildness I had learned to ride, gripped between my knees. So, horses were our first order of business when we arrived, carsick and travel grubby from our long haul across the country in the family station wagon, over the Vaal River and into the storybook I'd been telling her about all year. She could ride, but dressage and show jumping were her comfort zone; farm horses with their unpredictable manners, having generally been broken in just enough to make do, required something of a driver's ed class.

My father is her driving instructor; I am the student driver demonstrating how to manage the moody, sweaty horsepower at a safe speed. I saddle Sherry and check her girth, making sure she hasn't huffed her big belly out to trick me into a few extra inches of breathing room. My dad is at my shoulder as I dig my knee into her gut, butting her belly and cinching the girth tighter. I can hear his voice in my head, telling the familiar tall tale of how riders who fall for the bluff of a horse's puffed-out gut find their saddles slip sliding away once their horse exhales with their first fast steps. I live in fear of the humiliation of getting slung upside down because of a too-loose girth, proof of city slicker naïveté.

Once Sherry is bridled and saddled up, I put the toe of my left riding boot into the stirrup and launch myself up, swinging a leg over her back and searching for the right stirrup, checking the stirrup leathers for length as I settle into the warmth of her back, the sun hot on the saddle.

My dad looks up from under the brim of his hat and says, "Okay, take her up to the *Draai* and back and I'll follow with Nicole."

I nod and wheel the great chestnut out of the saddling paddock and toward the narrow pedestrian gate and the road beyond up to the *Draai*. I am playing it cool, but my heart is racing, and out of the corner of my eye I watch Nicole watching me. My shoulders are squared and my back is straight, the sun crisping through the crisscross straps on my eighties paint splatter shirt. I proudly navigate opening and closing the gate on horseback and start off at a slow trot, the ground under us packed hard and compact from a long rainless season. My dad and Nicole have to take the long way around in the car, and I know their road will intersect with the trail I'm following like two arms of an upside-down letter *Y* converging in the red dust.

As the green station wagon pulls level with me, I pick up speed, ready to put Sherry through her paces for my audience. I cluck at her, squeeze with my thighs, and urge her forward. But I have forgotten that she is wilier than I am, and she knows that I'm all show and no match for a strength usually held in check by the calloused hands and weight of grown men at work in the saddle rather than on vacation there.

She pulls away from my soft hands and clamps down on the bit, and I feel her muscles bunch and launch beneath me as the polite canter erupts into a frantic gallop. Rocks and earth and scrubby saltbush are a blur under my feet that have lost their grip on the stirrups, now flinging wildly unmanned at Sherry's sides. I have also lost the reins as the pace of the gallop shudders through my whole body, and I have stopped caring what I look like and care only about not coming into contact with the hard packed earth staring up startlingly close to me as each lunge of her flying legs flings me farther and farther down her neck.

I'm completely out of the saddle now, legs like zip ties trying to keep me attached to her lunging neck, fisting my fingers in her tawny mane, its long fringes flying back in the air and catching me across the eyes, the mouth, as we fly like one, a creature melded together by speed and terror. She veers off the road and into the veld, and the milking corral is a blur as we pass it, the staff houses also a flash as I glance over my shoulder to see my father's car flying low and fast over the rutted road as no station wagon was ever meant to do.

I don't have the breath to cry or yell or even pray, I'm just a heartbeat trying not to come untethered from a body. Nicole's face is a pale blur in the passenger's side window, her eyes massive, as my dad mouths at me from the distance. But the wind is so loud in my ears, it sucks his words away and he looks like a fish, opening and closing his impotent mouth as part of my brain desperately wonders how they will get me out of this mess. Instead, we keep flying, the horse and the car, until the horse runs out of steam first. Sherry slows her pace enough that I snatch my chance to slide off her neck and make a jump for the passing ground, like I have seen people do as they jump out of train boxcars when the engine slows at a crossing, timing it just right so that they don't lose their footing. I slide/jump off and she slows enough at the awkward shift in weight that I can grab at her reins and pull her to a stop.

I stand with my legs trembling, the dull yellow earth like an angry sea still lurching beneath me. I struggle to hold myself up, the horse heaving beside me as the green station wagon pulls up and my father bursts from the car. I am holding in the wild tears and gasps that I know will unleash the moment I feel safe, grown-up arms around me. I am ready for someone else to be in charge again so I can crawl back into my twelve-year-old self and cry while he tells me how brave I was to have ridden that wildness without coming apart at the seams.

I am rooted to the earth as my father runs toward me. His hat has fallen off, and I notice that his own hair looks wild and windswept. I lean forward until his words blow me back: "What the hell? What the bloody hell do you think you're doing?!"

I retreat while remaining dead still.

"How dare you? Dammit. How dare you risk a horse like that? Who do you think you are racing like that? You know, you KNOW better than to race over the rocks that damn fast. You could have broken her leg with your showing off!"

I stand facing my father as my muscles slowly lose all their strength, and I don't know how to translate the obvious for him.

Nicole has followed from the car, and from behind him her

words emerge like a white flag: "I don't think she was racing for fun."

His face is red and he has snatched the reins from me, as his hands soothe over Sherry's coat, now slick with sweat.

Nicole continues as my dad's hands run over Sherry's legs, "I think she nearly fell off. She wasn't in the saddle."

My shame is now my only hope.

My father is still panting but slowly seems to put the pieces of the puzzle together. My eyes are hot with tears and my cheeks aching from the wind and the determination not to let out my howl for comfort.

Instead, I nod as he changes tack and says, "Oh, okay. That's why you have to show her who's boss. Here, get back on." And he launches me back into the saddle, firmly setting each of my feet back into the stirrups himself. As he makes his way back to the car, he barks instructions over his shoulder, "Get a tight grip on the reins! Keep your knees locked on her. Just walk. Just walk back."

I turn the great horse, and the sky rotates above us as we move together alongside the car, her neck high and proud, my shoulders tired and humbled. My father marches us both home from the rolled-down window of his car. I unsaddle and let the horse loose while Nicole watches. Her silence isn't like the awkwardness between the moment when you get launched out of a saddle and hit the ground. Her silence is the moment of recognition when you spot someone you know across all the other heads in a crowded restaurant. She knows. I have sat in her bedroom while her own father misunderstands and belittles her at the top of his lungs in the hallway. I am known by her.

We walk into the house to wash up for tea. My muscles ache and I won't ever mention to anyone the bruising across and below my pubic bone from straddling the withers of a runaway charger. This is how I introduce her to our farm story.

* * *

A year later she and I will spend one summer selling brownies and cookies and raffle tickets for our own homemade prizes to raise enough money for two train tickets back to Middelburg. We will return without my family, just two tall, gangly, only-barely-turned-teen girls, picked up at the station by one of Auntie Christine's sons, to spend a week or two on the farm we have been dreaming about ever since we left. It's funny how the stories we tell ourselves about the people and places we love are written in glitter pens and decorated with puffy heart stickers, while there are no pages in the scrapbooks of our memories that have the photos of our falls or fears or shame.

We lean out the train windows, mouths gritty with dirt and dust, as mile after mile of the Great Karoo chugs past us. I clatter back through history, and my story intersects with my father's, who, at age seven, began his ritual migrations back and forth by train between the farm and the boarding school. As we disembark with our backpacks and excitement, I breeze past the ghost of my childhood father, who would beg on the platform, tears biting in the corners of his eyes, for his mother not to make him leave. Nicole and I are scouring the platform for our ride, and I don't see the small boy in his school uniform and green and white boater hat, pleading with his mother for time—always for more time on the farm—and she firmly leading him to the steps up and into the train car with young William from the neighboring farm. Two boys shipped off to school with mutton sandwiches wrapped in wax paper to hug their tiny tummies, the last taste of home for the next ten-week term.

Being shipped off to boarding school became the bogey-man my father would threaten us kids with. We didn't know what had happened there. We just knew we didn't want it to happen to us.

Nicole and I walk across my father's *spoor,* and I don't see it, even as I step into his childish excitement at being home. Sometimes his parents would have a business reason to travel the mountain passes to the town of Graaff-Reinet, the fourth oldest in South Africa, where his boarding school had been educating boys since 1919. My dad says those visits were al-most worse than the goodbyes at the train station. They were an unexpected bounty in the midst of the desert of homesick-ness, and it was almost more than he could bear to be deliv-ered back to the hostel after an afternoon of chicken pie and Fanta Orange with his parents. That is when he'd beg in ear-nest, "Please, Dad. Please, please take me home with you."

And his father would turn his bald sunburned head round in the car and snap over his shoulder, "Stop it. Stop it right now or next time I'm in town we won't come and visit you."

And my tiny father would slurp back his tears and drag his green blazer sleeve across his nose and say goodbye again from drowning eyes. My dad spent the entirety of his childhood try-ing to get home to the farm and then most of his adulthood trying to leave it.

* * *

That solo train trip with Nicole at age thirteen was one of the last holidays to the farm that I remember before I turned sixteen and leukemia came for my mother. All future trips were reduced to the one between our home in Pretoria and my mother's hospital room in Johannesburg.

The next time we cram into the green station wagon to make the trip down to the farm, I've just turned eighteen and we are towing a trailer behind us carrying my mom in her coffin. We drive miles and miles, farther and farther away from the civilized grief of her memorial service in South Africa's capital city, and deeper into the wildest parts of the country where our family's raw history opens up like a wound cutting across the great heart of the Karoo.

We pause at the Orange River, walking down to kneel at its banks, the water still singing the same song of hope in a dry land as it did when my dad was a teen canoeing its entire length with his best friend—thirty-two days it took them to ride its 1,200 miles across the country. They made headlines at the time. It is cold now. Spring hasn't quite arrived here yet.

The day of my mom's funeral we are guests on our own farm, wearing our awkwardness like visitor badges. The house with its ancient groans and creaks is no longer a member of our family. The land traded for the cost of bone marrow transplants and eighteen months of hospital stays and several more of brutal hospice care. All we have retained are the burial rights up in *Meerkat Vlaktes*, Meerkat Plains.

I have picked out one of my mom's own outfits to wear to her funeral. The blue blouse with the little white paisley pattern has shoulder pads too wide for my eighteen-year-old frame. The palazzo pants threaten to fall down and pool around my ankles. I roll the waist over and over again. My mom's generous roundness was always my favorite comfort. It has been years since she was able to fill out these clothes. We are both too skinny for them at the end.

I am bleeding on the day she is buried. It's as if my womanhood is weeping. I haven't packed tampons or pads and so I will have to tell my father that we need to stop at the small pharmacy in Middelburg before we drive the curve of the road past the Black township with its broken lights and out into the vast farmland where his grief is waiting to swallow him whole. I speak three languages, but I can't find the words to tell him what I need. I can't remember what excuse I use to beg the man already running late to bury his wife to pull into the parking spot outside the glass windows lined with their aspirin bottles, shampoos, and Johnson's Baby Cream. But stop he does, and me and my awkward shoulders slink down the aisles for a final moment with my mother as I pick out pads and pay for them with my father's money. I have lost my mother. I have lost my interpreter of womanhood.

* * *

It is like a ridiculous cosmic joke, how God has taken the parent that wears comfort as easily as my mother did—the roundness of extra pounds that never embarrassed her—and left me with the one who sees any evidence of extra weight as proof of sloth and the sin of lack of self-discipline. I shout this at God one night. I shout like my father shouts, sitting on the curb of the driveway outside our house, under the arch of an acacia tree, both of us transplanted far from our roots on the farm. I shout that He has got it wrong and, "What were You *thinking*, God? What could You possibly have been thinking to have taken my mother and left me with my *father?*"

I am as furious and impotent as I can ever remember being.

The Southern Cross bears witness to my bleak rage, and I sit on the little ledge of the curb, picking at the pods that litter our driveway and the street. Acacia trees don't just produce a crop of thorns. Yellow flowers like cotton balls sprout on their prickly branches and are followed by seedpods like long fingers that ripen and turn from green to brown until they let go their branches and helicopter to the ground. They line the driveway of what used to be my mom's dream house. She always wanted a home with an open floor plan where the kitchen flowed into the living room and into the yard beyond. This was hers for three years before she got sick, and my memories fall as fast and sticky as the dry seedpods.

I remember her in this driveway wearing her little sea-green nightie–sleep shirt dancing a jig while Dad loaded us all up in the car for school. She'd laugh and dance, her white limbs flashing a semaphore of joy as she waved her dramatic goodbyes. She was weirdly wonderful, and we loved every bit of it.

I remember sprinting down this driveway the day I got my first period. I was so furious that my body would try to sideline me during track season that I was determined to prove nothing could slow me down. So after my mom explained to me what had happened, I explained to her that it would have zero impact on my speed, my training, my wind sprints.

I remember yanking up the garage door and launching myself out and down this driveway, pedaling my bike hell-for-leather, as my father's screams followed me down the road and around the corner. My mom was in the hospital by then, and I was trying to plan a birthday surprise for a boy from church I had a crush on. I'd left the planning to the last minute, as was my way. I wanted it to be epic, and so I had asked my father if I could gift the boy my dad's precious Chinese dragon kite. It was a glorious one hundred meters of Mylar crafted to look like stained glass art that danced and roared in the wind. My father had been hoarding the kite for years; I couldn't remember if he'd ever used it. And I was desperate for a gift that would impress a fifteen-year-old boy.

It was a mistake. I had stepped on a landmine, and it exploded with the familiar shock of unpredictability. My father was shaking with rage. "You're too damn lazy to plan ahead? And now, now you want *my* kite?"

I shook my head. "No, no, it's okay; I shouldn't have asked."

I was backing away from him as he stood out of his chair where he was reading the New Testament in Greek and started advancing on me. "What a cheek! It's a damn cheek, you know?"

He was following me out of his study as I held up my hands in surrender, waving away the flames that I could see I'd set; they were licking at me now, and I knew the building was unstable.

"It's fine, Dad, I have a card and balloons. I don't need a present."

"You're damn right you don't! I can't believe you wait till the night before I have a big day at work and now I'm supposed to just fix this for you? I'm supposed to just drop everything and drive you *and give* you *my* kite?"

We're down the hallway now and headed to the garage. I no longer imagine myself asking him for a ride.

"No, it's okay, Dad. Sorry. I'll just take my bike. It's fine."

My heart is roaring in my ears, and I know we have seconds, just seconds before the floor crumbles.

"Get out! Just get out of my sight! You're so damn selfish. Get out!"

He grabs my bike and throws it at me in the narrow sliver of space between the two parked cars. I grab it with my burning hands and try to twist it around, try to twist myself around to get out.

"*Voetsek!*" he yells at me in the language we use for disobedient dogs. "Get lost! Get out! GO!" His words are licking at my heels as I launch myself on the bike and down the road and into the twilight. I cry and pedal and swallow, and the wind is a balm on my fiery cheeks.

I remember my first kiss in this driveway. For a full twelve months of my mother's hospitalization I had been getting roses from an anonymous admirer. I remember the first time the doorbell rang and I discovered the bouquet. It was yellow. My dad was next door with the neighbors. It was a summer night and I opened the front door to the blossoms and warm air crept in like a hug. The roses and cards with their stenciled notes of encouragement, of admiration continued through the summer and fall and winter and spring. The whole time my mother was dying, a beautiful anonymous love story was blooming on my doorstep.

I called him the *Phantom Rose*. At night his roses would arrive, and during the day the high school swim star started paying me attention. But I was so awkward in my grief, my whole world felt as pale as my white, white legs—a stark contrast to the vibrant tans of my friends who were practicing their sunbathing and eyeliner while I was practicing how to cook for our family and staying healthy so I would be allowed to visit my mother with her compromised immune system. I couldn't conceive of a world where the most popular boy in school would be interested in me beyond a passing politeness because my best girlfriend was one of his best friends. But every week I'd hear the purr of a 250cc motorbike that heralded the arrival of another flower delivery, and while the boy who drove a bike just like that to school was the subject of my daydreams he never featured in my reality.

Until the day during recess when he outed himself, and I don't know who was more shocked, him or me. I remember how that afternoon he came to the house and for the first time in twelve months didn't run after ringing the doorbell. He stood there as beautiful in his leather jacket as he was in the pool. He'd taken out all his piercings because he thought he'd be meeting my father for the first time. He didn't know that my father was always working. And we were always home alone. We were always some degree of lonely. But he must have known. My Phantom Rose. He'd seen through the watery smiles to the center of me, and roses had been his love language. He'd been loving me in pink and yellow and white, in orange and blush and lush maroon. And somehow in an impossible season I'd blossomed because of this boy.

For our first date that weekend I wore lilac jeans, knee-high black boots, and an off-the-shoulder black top. That night my father was home, and the Phantom Rose introduced himself and informed my dad that the party he'd been planning to take me to wasn't a good idea after all.

"Sir, I just don't think it's the kind of party I want to take Lisa-Jo to."

I'd been desperate to have him pull me away onto the back of his motorbike and into another world. But he was firm. "I think it would be better if we just hung out here."

My dad shook his hand and welcomed him into the house.

But I was in a panic because my bedroom told the full story of how deep my feelings ran for him, outfit after outfit tried on and rejected and left dejected on the bedroom floor. I was scrambling to pick up tank tops and shorts and jeans and shove them under the bed, into the closet, anywhere to get them out of his sight. But he saw everything, and I was swimming in deep waters now; I saw for the first time what it feels like to catch a glimpse of yourself reflected in the view of someone who loves you. I made him a mug of hot chocolate. I didn't know where to sit. I ended up crisscross applesauce on my bed, with its girly pink duvet cover. He sat at my desk, long legs that barely fit in my small space. His words warmed the places the hot chocolate had missed.

I don't know what we talked about. I didn't know that this would be our only date. I didn't know that I would lose the ability to speak to this boy after tonight. I didn't know that my feelings for him would collide with my grief, my rage, my responsibilities in this house and that I would have no mother to teach me how to talk to the first boy I ever loved. I didn't know that I would break his heart and push him away with my own paralyzing tsunami of contradictory experiences all crammed into my junior year of high school. I didn't know that I would always regret how I treated this boy after tonight. But on that South African summer evening we experienced a singular sacred moment, a time outside of time.

When we were done with our hot chocolate and our conversation, he walked back out of the bedroom and down the hallway to shake my father's hand in his study, and I told my dad I'd walk the Phantom Rose out. The jasmine was waiting for us. I could barely breathe it was so heavy in the air, and I desperately needed to get more oxygen into my lungs because

I was so lightheaded. He walked over to the motorbike I had spent months listening for. He didn't get on. He simply leaned against it and opened his arms and I stepped into them. I had no idea what I was doing. The shiver started low in my spine as he tightened his wingspan around me, and then he was kissing me.

And in that moment, I moved from death to life, from grief to elation, from shyness to a wild confidence I didn't know lived inside me. I reached my arms up, up, up and my head back, back, back and welcomed this boy's love into myself. Everything became the opposite of my life—warm, safe, beautiful, wanted, beloved, cherished. I experienced the kiss like the taste of jasmine, the drunkenness of the stars spinning me dizzy behind my eyes, the darkness wrapping us both up in its embrace, innocent and hidden away from pain, from our reputations, from our families' expectations. He was not the bad boy and I was not the good girl. We were two stems intertwined, trading our thorns for a burst of bright yellow buds.

The kiss lasted and lasted, and I hoped I was doing it right until he pulled his head back and breathed in a deep gasp of air, resting his chin on the top of my head and exhaling these words into my ear: "I've waited a whole year for that."

He paused, then followed with, "It was worth it."

My chest exploded with pleasure and an unfamiliar sense of power.

My cheek was pressed against his rib cage, and we were breathing together and I didn't realize I'd said it out loud: "Your heart is racing."

He chuckled, nodded, pulled me in closer, his thick blond hair falling across his face, and I could feel it across my temple, this holy moment of oneness.

We stood there a long time, the swimmer and the girl he had saved from drowning.

When I went back inside, my father was sitting in the lounge, a glass of sherry in his hand. It was cut crystal, a small flute of amber liquid. He was watching TV and looked up as I walked in. He didn't say anything. He didn't comment on my flushed cheeks. He didn't question my hair that was surely now all a tangle of fingers and feelings. He simply reached over and handed me a second glass of sherry that I saw then had been waiting for me. I took the delicate glass and his gentle offering of knowing. His recognition that something had changed in his daughter. The air vibrated between us with all the words we weren't saying. And I received it like a gift. I swallowed the sweet liquid, and it burned down my throat and pooled in my belly. This moment of recognition, of transformation heralded by my father without saying a single word. We lingered over our drinks; it was a lighthouse kind of night.

CHAPTER 5

Once Upon a Terrible Time

A year after that first kiss, I hear that my swimmer got his first tattoo. A delicate rose near his hip bone. But by then I have lost my all-access pass to his story, his lips, his hips. I live in an underwater world now where I can't breathe because we are all just waiting for my mother to die. I could tell you what it feels like to be seventeen with a dying mother. It feels like you're not sure how hard to study for that final math exam because waiting for death turns out to be exhausting, and won't it provide you with the perfect excused absence anyway? It feels like spring is bullying you, laughing at the smell of your mother's hospice room. It feels like the moment between the dentist's shot of novocaine and his drill. It feels like unfairness.

In August I turn eighteen. In September my mom dies. In December I graduate high school, and by January I'm on a plane headed overseas. America, Canada, Holland, Germany, England—a gap-year pilgrimage to connect the dots in my mother's family tree, visiting the branches I know only from the frames on our wall. But then, in February, my father calls to tell me he's engaged. And by May he will be remarried to a woman I've never met.

I'm in Philadelphia for his announcement. I'm in Germany for his wedding day.

I can tell you what it feels like to be a motherless daughter and a stepdaughter in the same twelve months. It feels like nausea, like drowning while the lifeguard is grinning at you from above the water as his hand pushes your head down, down, down.

In Philadelphia I am staying with the same pastor and his wife who had known, loved, welcomed my young parents to the States as visiting grad students fifteen years earlier. I was in kindergarten with their son. They are still grieving my mother's death. I am upstairs when the mom calls to me that my dad is on the phone. I'm bursting with excitement to share with him my first impressions of his America. I clutch the cordless phone and feel the soft, warm caramel carpet under my feet as I climb back up the stairs two at a time to my bedroom and privacy for this walk down memory lane with my father. But he speaks first. "I've got some wonderful news."

I'm so happy for him. Happy that there are still wonderful things in the world available to my father. Happy that I don't have to keep feeling guilty for leaving.

"God has sent the most amazing woman into my life. It's like a miracle."

My reaction is immediate and visceral. Fear like nausea slams into my solar plexus so hard I find myself working my jaw, trying to release the pressure I feel building there. I don't remember the other words he uses to describe his crushing new love and their wedding plans. What I remember is the sunshine filtering in through the ice frozen like lace over the second-floor bedroom windows and how familiar the fear feels. That sense of instability and unpredictability that had haunted me for the eighteen months of my mom's cancer, that had lain dormant for the few months since we'd buried her and I'd boarded a plane into her story, with the blessing of my father. Now I feel the creature rise in me again with the bile in my throat, hot and vicious and wide awake. "Dad, I'm glad you're doing better. But does this sound like a good idea? I'm worried. It's really soon, Dad."

And this is where he and I part ways. It wasn't at the airport after all. It was on Valentine's Day with all its superstition and tradition suspended between us on an international phone call. My father's grief acts like some kind of *sangoma,* a witch doctor that casts a spell over him and extracts all rational thought from his body. Like an exorcism, I watch as logic, patience, and ordinary sense are pulled out through his mouth with every word he speaks. Like a *djinn* leaving his body. Every syllable is an incantation against my mother and an indictment of anyone who doesn't embrace this vision for his future. This thing is what he wants, and he uses God's name to justify his choice. He takes God's name in literal vain, demanding we accept this shotgun relationship as God's will for all of us. He accuses me of being faithless if I fail to believe in this new woman.

Our phone call disintegrates in my hands. I can't coax him back into himself. I can't find the words to make him hear me, let alone understand me. We don't set even one foot down memory lane. Instead, we take a sharp detour and the navigation shifts into a language I don't understand and can't speak, and I am lost, so lost. The call escalates into accusations of disloyalty from him and astonishment from me as I learn that the wedding can't even wait for me to land back home again. He is unwilling to adjust his brand-new plans to accommodate the ones he and I had spent a year making together. He knows my itinerary down to the minute of each country until I touch back down in South Africa. And still he says, "I talked to the travel agent, and they can just bring you home earlier; it's not a big deal to change the ticket."

"But I'll miss out on seeing Mom's cousins in Germany." My voice is so thick I can barely swallow. My heart is racing, and I'm taking tiny breaths like a toddler who has wandered too far into a pool with its slowly sloping floor and realizes too late they've been walking themselves into the drowning end. And now the water is lapping around my neck, and I'm standing on desperate tippy-toes, tilting my head all the way back so my mouth and nose can still break the surface for the oxygen I'm terrified to see disappearing all around me. It's only a matter of time before I slip under.

He is a charging bull with only one thought in his mind. And he insists everyone will be happy for him. Will accommodate him. I shock us both by being unaccommodating for the first time in our relationship.

"Dad, you just met her. I have to finish this trip."

"Then you're going to miss the wedding!"

"I mean, you could wait till I'm home?"

"I thought you'd be happy for me!"

"Dad, Mom just died. I'm here with your oldest friends. I just got here. We haven't even had time to catch up yet really. About you and Mom. About your time here."

I'm reaching my hand up, up out of the water, sure he'll grab it and pull me out from under the blanket of beautiful, airless blue death.

He doesn't.

He tells me if I loved him, I'd come home.

He tells me if I loved Jesus, I'd be happy for him.

He doesn't tell me he loves me. He doesn't ask about my broken heart.

Happy Valentine's Day.

I sit with the receiver in my hands, and I'm crouching on the carpet, a small, wounded creature. A stranger in a strange land.

I don't know how to tell my host family about the phone call. Instead, I go down to breakfast and unwrap the beautiful Valentine's gift the mom has bought for me. She has included me along with her own teenage children in the all-American tradition of Valentine's Day gift baskets. It is surreal to me; I feel like I am watching a movie from the inside out. She hasn't just got me a card or bought me a box of chocolates or a quick cheapie gift from the dollar store. She's given me an expensive, lush pink, floor-length terrycloth bathrobe that wraps around me like a hug. Like a way to hide my naked shock and shame and grief even from myself. Thirty years later it is still the most unexpected luxury I've received from a near stranger.

I now have two competing griefs. The public grief of my dead mother and the secret grief of my father's dead marriage. I wear them like my own tattoo, a double helix of thorn branches. On Valentine's night the teenagers invite me out with them; they're going to the Gap.

"The space?" I ask them.

"No." They're putting on lipstick, bootcut jeans, chunky shoes. "The Gap. You know, that store at the mall."

I don't know. So I have no idea what to wear.

"Is this too smart?" I call down the hallway to the bathroom, and one pops a head out, looking at me in confusion.

"Too smart?"

"Yes, like too fancy or something." I try to translate my meaning.

"Oh. Like preppy?"

I nod my head on the outside and shake it on the inside. Their phrase is foreign to me.

"No, you're good."

I don't know how much money to bring. In South Africa I'd bring a hundred rand, but they tell me twenty dollars should do it here. I'm nervous. I stuff a traveler's check into my jeans just in case, along with the twenty-dollar bill. We don't go to the Gap. I still don't know what it is. Instead, we sit in a car on the night of Valentine's Day in the frozen cold of a Philadelphia side street parking lot. The crowded breathing of our teenage bodies fogs up the windows. The pastor's son and daughters and friends and I are all sardined into this tiny space, and I'm a legal alien who doesn't speak the language. Their tape deck hums along with the nervous energy in the car, and I laugh too, wishing we were at the mall instead. Wishing I knew what was going on. But I don't know what cool sounds like in their culture. I've never spoken it in my own.

They roll down the windows a crack, and I realize we're parked here to watch men come and go from the two-story building across the way. It takes a long time for the word they're passing around like a shared cigarette to fill my lungs and come out my lips. "Johns?" Is that really what they said? What we are sitting here watching? Middle-aged men moving through this back lot with their anonymous cash, their desperation to numb their lives with someone else's body? Have teenagers raised on the ancient language of faith, hope, and love really settled for gawking at the facsimile? Is this how we're spending our Valentine's? I sit and watch men my father's age slip into a door in a building I can barely make out through the condensation on the car windows.

Everything is a fog. Nothing makes sense to me anymore.

Weeks later I am in Canada as part of my pilgrimage through my mom's family and friends. I stay with the church friends who used to live down the road from us in South Africa. It's the closest I can get to trying to go home to my life before my mom died. He was the young and fiery American preacher who had transplanted his family to follow "the call to Africa" until they got too homesick. They were the ones who had opened their sliding door to the shock and snot and tears running down our faces on the night we found out about my mom's diagnosis. They had made tea and made a nightmare bearable. Now they have followed the call to Canada and the baby girl I used to babysit is a curious preschooler. I remember her baby shower. I remember she was the first baby I ever babysat for. I remember my mom dropping me off, and all twenty pounds of baby chub toddling toward me and wrapping her baby arms around my neck, pressing her sweet baby breath against my cheek.

Now her tears scream out of her as her mother pulls her down across her knee. I watch as the mom spanks and spanks and spanks her tiny daughter. Like my father, they take Proverbs 13:24, "Whoever spares the rod hates their children," literally. I don't know where to look. Her mom catches my eye across the wails and tears, and she shrugs. "It stops bothering you after a while."

In Holland I stay in the attic of my mom's great-aunt. I get violently sick. Everything inside has now pushed its way outside. It's the first and last time in my life I have to use a chamber pot because I am too weak to make it up or down all the narrow stairs. My fog is heavy and thick now. They take me to a doctor, and I speak Afrikaans to his Dutch. It turns out I have a yeast infection on top of everything else. These are not easy things to communicate in the presence of strangers in any language. I lie in my attic room in Utrecht and don't realize the kind of love I am receiving that climbs the stairs to clean out my pot twice a day. My mother's people mother me. They are in their sixties, but I am the one bent over and aching. I age years in those months from February to May. Every stop I make I have to break the news of my father's impending marriage. Shame and grief sweat out my pores in the narrow bed where I lie in my flaming pain.

But they want to show me their country. The birthplace of the beautiful bookshelves and bureaus and *brei*, that ability to trill the letter *r*, that my mother had inherited. So, as I start to recover, they take me to visit the tulip fields, the impressionist museums, the theater. And I become a blurry, heavy brush stroke in a van Gogh painting. Everything is overwhelming, and my two stories of loss are splitting me down the middle.

In Germany my mother's cousins take me into their homes, lives, Easter egg hunts. They know so much more about her than I do. Before I even arrive, my great-aunt and uncle have once again tended their grandniece by calling ahead and spreading my father's news through the rest of the family grapevine. I imagine those conversations running down the line from English to Dutch to German. So my second cousins are tender with the teenager who sleeps too much and spends too much on her father's credit card. It is the only way she has to hurt him back.

They take me on a trip to the Black Forest, and I savor that name in my mouth; in English those words taste like rich, gooey, decadent, dark chocolate cake with ganache and chocolate shavings garnishing each bite. In German the *Schwarzwald* syllables sound like the borderland between our world and the universe of magic, where trees can tell tall tales and fairies are just as real as the cuckoo clocks taking flight in the tens of thousands from the region. Time becomes fluid and I am suspended between my past life and my future life.

My father is sorry I'm not at the wedding. He's not sorry about the wedding. And he's not sorry enough to wait. He finds my sadness unreasonable and my refusal to be happy for him rebellious. More than that, I think he finds the mirror of me too difficult to look into. I reflect my mother's name, which is stitched right into the third syllable of my own.

I take a day trip to Paris. We're only a train ride away and my host family urges me to get out, to explore, to adventure. Also, I think it's likely a relief to have the couch surfer out of the house for a brief moment of exhale. I go to Paris alone. I wear white jeans and a sea-green sweater and a European-style pageboy cap. I desperately want to look stylish, fashionable, the opposite of myself. I navigate the train schedule in German, and then the subway map in French. There is no one to take my photo; you can't take a selfie with an old point-and-shoot. I wait in line for hours with the throbbing throng of pilgrims committed to making it to the top of the Eiffel Tower.

There is a couple waiting next to me. We are all pressed

together in the elevator cage. It is hot and sweaty. He holds on to her like a climbing vine, slips his hand down her thigh, slides his tongue into her mouth; they French-kiss at the bottom and the top and every stage in between of Paris's most romantic landmark. I watch them more than I should. Furtively from below the brim of my cap. I watch how his hands are hungry for her. I watch how she leans, willowlike, toward him. They are like one breath. They belong to each other. They impact me more than the tower does.

I am still thinking about them at two A.M. on a train platform in Strasbourg, France, waiting for my connecting train back to Freiburg, Germany. I am starting to become confused by the conflagration of languages. I keep my sight trained on the flickering yellow eyes of the electric sign counting down the minutes till my train's arrival. The station manager has told me not to miss this train, since it's the last straggler of the night. Across from me a big beast has pulled in, chugging loud in the silence like a runner catching its breath. Backpackers come and go. Tickets are handed over. And still I sit, just watching. My train isn't supposed to be here yet. The station is emptying out.

I am alone.

There is no cellphone, no mother, no father, no lover, no tour guide, no safety net.

I don't belong to anyone.

There are no hands holding me, anchoring me, loving me.

I am alone and adrift.

I try to translate the announcement pounding in my head over the loudspeakers. The air is muggy and the voice very hard to follow. Something comes to me from deep in my heartbeat. Like a parent urging a toddler to take a first step.

My brain rallies and I slowly stand, walk to the train to try to decode the words on the train's destination information. It enters my eyes in German and has to be rerouted through my brain's German centers, my Afrikaans and Dutch files offering aid, before it can be translated into fragments of English. And as the conductor starts to bellow his all aboard, the connections fire and I realize this might be my train. I feel myself start to run. I rush to the far door where the conductor is and yell at him in German, "Is this the train to Freiburg?"

"Yes, jump. Now!" he yells back.

I grab the door handle and my feet make it on board as the beast slowly starts its long crawl out of the station. My heart is jabbering at high speed as I rock unsteadily through the passenger car and into a cabin with a door I can close. Three A.M. now, and still I am alone. I hear the European equivalent of frat boys laughing and swearing through the walls, and I turn my face to the window. The world is darkness beyond; the window is a mirror now, and I try not to make eye contact with my reflection. I feel like the last person left awake in this in-between land. My hope that the compartment stays empty is a prayer that wings its way out onto the rails and becomes the sound of each stitch and clack of the tracks.

I am alone but also I am not alone.

I hear the small, still voice that beats in my chest. A heartbeat that seems to speak an ancient language to my soul, that keeps drumming into me my next right step, interpretation, connection. I am learning to trust the unspoken language of faith that floods my veins, no longer transfused from my parents but produced at the cellular level in my own body.

I cannot remember if I actually talked to my dad on his wedding day or not. I do remember that my mom's youngest sister attended with her husband and my cousins. Their love for her and her branch in the family tree carried them through what I can only imagine read like a Grimm Brothers cliché. My aunt is a librarian after all, gatekeeper and experienced guide through the land of fairy tale.

They attend a wedding just over half a year since her sister died. There is a determined stepmother who wants a new house and the title of "doctor's wife," which she casually inserts into every conversation as she describes the family and new life she is building for her only child. There is a literal horse-drawn Cinderella-style carriage, a new castle-like house built into the side of a mountain, and a wedding dress that would have made Princess Diana blush. They tell me afterward that my father cried during his speech at the glittering evening reception, saying how much he wished his daughter could have been there.

In London I stay with the spinster who is something between fairy godmother and grandmother to my parents. She tucks me into a small back bedroom and feeds me from the copious notes taken during the cooking shows she obsessively watches. I'm there long enough to get a job in the West End, where stories live and breathe and have their being. Night after night the Andrew Lloyd Webber musical numbers performed on roller skates and the insane costumes seep into my bloodstream like an intravenous joy drip. It catches me by surprise. The front-of-house staff in their cheeky, lilting British accents invite me to their local pub. I learn it's the closest thing to being invited into their homes. Night after night the cast members meet us there after belting out the big finale, "The Light at the End of the Tunnel," and signing autographs at the stage door. I'm a tourist who doesn't like the taste of Guinness but savors the flavor of belonging again.

I am eighteen and I don't want to go home.

* * *

At eighteen all my father wanted to do was leave home. He negotiated hard with his own father for permission to leave the farm and study medicine. His dad countered with veterinary science, which would at least have been helpful on a farm.

"If you study medicine, the farm can't go to you," Grandpa said.

"Okay, that's okay with me, Dad, but I'm not going to study vet."

My father came by his love of medicine honestly. One of Grandpa's brothers had been obsessed with medicine, with understanding how the mechanics of veins and arteries, lungs and heart work. Back then they'd host baboon hunts for him and his best friend so the two could Frankenstein their own anatomy labs. In an unrefrigerated farm shed, they'd inject the dead animals with dye, coloring the arteries red and the veins blue so they could study and understand the mysteries of what makes life tick. They'd preserve the great carcasses with formaldehyde and then spend weeks dissecting them on the farm until Grandpa said the stench had become unbearable. But this brother, my dad's uncle, would grow up to be the Chief of Surgery at the prestigious University of Cape Town Medical School, and his friend and farm anatomy lab partner would eventually rise to curator of the London Zoo.

"If you fail out of medical school, you have to come back and farm with me," Grandpa bargained with my dad.

"If I pass, then can I go on studying? Will you keep paying?"

"Yes," Grandpa agreed. He would keep paying.

Grandpa was in his seventies by then and had already weathered multiple heart attacks. His youngest son was home between graduating high school and starting at the University of Cape Town himself and had all the arrogance of the heir and very little of the proven experience.

Grandpa was running the farm from his bedroom, where he managed his angina and his staff from the double bed that faced the windows. There were no screens in the frames, and the men stopped by throughout the day to give him updates through the open window: reports on the sheep, the weather, the *mealies*. Grandpa sat propped up against the pillows reading over stock prices, the weather reports, the agricultural news. His Bible was a new addition to his nightstand.

A flock of eight hundred ewes needed to be dosed— standard protocol for control of internal parasites—and my dad told Grandpa he could manage it, could manage the men and the dust and the heat and the lives of their livestock. He was determined to show his father how fast he could get it done. But there is nothing quick about sheep dosing.

The flock had been herded into a *kraal,* or sheep pen, packed in tight, all eight hundred bleating voices on a perpetual loop, their wool a dingy white, droppings and urine on constant repeat, hooves scrabbling at the ground, sometimes at each other as a frantic ewe scrambled for a better spot and mounted her two forelegs up on the back of the sheep in front, straining for escape.

The day started early and loud. My dad's second-in-command was called Job, as in "work," not the Bible character. The sheep were herded toward the narrowest part of the pen, the crush, where they could easily be caught, jaws forced open, and the drench gun with its long spout shoved down the sheep's throat, the dose of medicine pumped out, like squeezing a gas pump. Dad was pumping the drench like a motocross racer pumps his gas. Always accelerating. Eight hundred sheep will take you all day. Green mucus coats your jeans, and the dust and dirt coat your nose, your hair, the inside of your throat and eyelids.

I've only ever watched sheep dosing from a perch on the top rung of a fence—never big enough to be in the thick of the crushing action. It is hot, backbreaking, soul-crushing work. With only two hundred still to go, Job materialized at my father's frantic elbow and announced, *"Kleinsir, die skape lê.* Small sir, the sheep are lying down."

My dad paused, looked up, wiped sweat and dirt and manure out of his eyes, and said, *"What?"*

Job looked at him with his shepherd's eyes. And my father saw himself reflected back, the picture of a hired hand who didn't realize his speed and force were causing the sheep to aspirate on the medicine as it bubbled back up from the stomach into the esophagus. He dropped the drench gun and watched Job, who started kneeling on the chests of his sheep that had blown up like balloons, giving them a kind of CPR, trying to force up what was choking them and get air back into their lungs. My dad joined him, while all around them sheep were gurgling and dying with medicine pouring out of their noses and flies squatting in the corners of their eyes.

They lost twenty-three before they could start back up dosing the rest. They went slower then. More men were called in to help with the late afternoon shift. And slowly, slowly it was finished. My father was there till the very end and didn't come home until the shadows were long, pointy, wagging fingers across the side of the house. He walked disheveled, crestfallen, and ashamed into his dad's bedroom. What he didn't know was that Job had already slipped off ahead and reported the whole sorry day to Grandpa through the bedroom window. Maybe he hoped to take the sting out of the old man's reaction. The shepherd who lacked the vocabulary of authority to correct the son was perhaps more familiar, even more comfortable, with the language of rebuke from the father.

"Yes, and, how did it go?" My grandfather sat up in bed, a pillow behind his back, the distant sounds of sheep carrying across the vast Karoo and into the room.

"Really badly." My father wiped his hand across his face, leaned against the doorframe, exhaled.

"Why? Didn't you finish?" Sharp blue eyes watched him.

"We finished but I didn't dose well. I was in a hurry, and we lost some sheep."

"How many?"

My dad looked out the window. He reeked of farming. He dreamed of medicine.

"Eighteen."

"Twenty-three actually," Grandpa responded.

My dad's head jerked up.

"Job already told me," said the old farmer.

When my dad tells me the story decades later, he says softly, under his breath, "I felt so betrayed at that moment."

"Yes," he answered his father, "it probably was twenty-three if Job says so."

The cats were being fed on the other side of the house, and the frogs in the reservoir outside the dining room were already raising their voices in their loud, lusty nightly chorus.

"What's happening to the dead sheep?" Grandpa asked.

"The men are skinning them and using whatever meat they can. They'll bring some down to the house for us too."

And then, my father would tell me, "Then I just wept." He sat down on the edge of his dad's bed, the soft quilt with its faded colors under him, head dropped on his chin, and let the tears come. And Grandpa put a hand on his son's shoulder and softly patted it and asked, "Well, what did you learn from this?"

And Dad replied in his hoarse voice, "I've got to be careful; I've got to go slowly. I must care for every animal, and every one is important."

Grandpa rubbed his beloved son between the shoulder blades. And said in his gravelly voice, "Now, that's a lesson I'm paying a lot of money for you to learn. Make sure you don't forget it."

* * *

I land back in South Africa six months after I left, and the earth comes rushing up to meet me faster than I'm ready for. I'm wearing charcoal jeans and boots from Holland, a belt from Germany, and a white bodysuit from London. The pink robe from Philly is packed in my suitcase. I am different. The two stories of death live inside me now. I wear them like a second skin. I am still not ready to be a character in this new story. Everything is moving too fast and I can't breathe.

My father is at the arrivals gate with his shotgun wife and my new teenage stepbrother. I am the sheep herded toward him whether I like it or not. My stepmother walks up to me and throws her arms around me. I get a mouthful of her lilac argyle sweater. I feel like I am choking as she announces in a rush, "I'm so excited to be your new mom!"

CHAPTER 6

Concussed

I am hiding in the house with my little brother. My seventeen-year-old stepbrother is at the front door. He is banging and screaming and swearing, and I am terrified. My father has called from work to warn me to get out. I only have my learner's permit. I can feel my own heartbeat like it's choking me, it's so high up in my throat. I look out the second-floor kitchen window of my father's wife's new house. This is where we live now. My mother's house with her beloved kitchen into living room into backyard, with the debauched bougainvillea dropping its lush magenta petals like discarded pieces of clothing across the lawn, was sold before I got back. And all the furniture from my childhood, along with her clothes, her jewelry, her scarves and shoes and handbags and the hot brush she used on her hair, are gone. My father has kept her books. My mother has been buried and then erased, and we now live in a house-castle built on the side of a mountain that is fit for a Hansel and Gretel stepmother. Or a doctor's wife.

She isn't home today. But her son is. The union of families has not gone well. I am not the only one resistant to the idea.

And I am not going to dissect how we got here—to the afternoon I am a hostage in this house and forcing myself to go downstairs to get the car keys that are hanging in my dad's study, with only the front door and its stubborn lock between me and the man-boy who is throwing fists and threats at the old wooden door with the sunburst pattern carved into it. My father is not here to protect us from the pressure cooker he moved into this house. We face it alone.

"Open the door! I know you're in there! Open it! Open it now!"

He's screaming and sobbing, and I hear the fleshy imprint of his fists over and over again on the doorframe as the handle rattles and rolls and shakes.

I'm in the front hall and I can see his outline through the mottled glass surrounding the front door. My hands are ice-cold as I lean into my dad's study, just steps away from the door, and slip the car keys off the row of hooks hanging on the wall. I back away from the entry, my shoulder blades twitching as I turn my back to the front door and make my knees that are stiff with fright bend and extend, bend and extend back up the stairs, avoiding the corners that creak, swallowing my own breaths, forcing myself to inhale even my tiniest sounds. My little brother is waiting in the kitchen. By the time I get back to him, I hear the front door crash open. Our stepbrother has a key, and he has persevered though the twists and turns of the infamously temperamental lock.

I am outside my body now. I watch myself slip open the bolt on the back door. I watch myself try to make words without making sounds. I watch myself lead my little brother out of the house around to the back steps. This is where my father has tried to grow a climbing garden. There are a fig tree and succulents, tall grasses, a small pond and burbling fountain and steps built out of slabs of rock. We take them two and three at a time. A branch whips my eye. We don't pause or slow or talk. We run.

My stepbrother is also running. I hear him crashing through the kitchen door and slamming it back and forth behind him in frustration before he dives after us. He isn't even trying to navigate the actual steps. He is simply launching himself off them. My dad's old green Volkswagen Passat station wagon is parked in the driveway. The keys are sweaty in my hand. This is not the first time my stepbrother has been violent.

We are inside the car now. I lock the doors and try to start the engine. It turns over and I put it into gear, but the clutch grinds and the gas jerks as my feet slip on the pedals, and my stepbrother is at my window. I do not look at him. But I can hear him, his screams piercing, loud, manic as he beats on my window. I focus on my hands on the steering wheel and tell my body to relax, to let muscle memory lead us through. Clutch, gas, ease up on the brake, trust the motions I've been through a hundred times before. My mouth is so dry I taste sandpaper. The screaming at my window is lessening as the car pulls forward and jerks down the driveway.

I look in the rearview mirror and he is running after us. His face is red and swollen with tears and rage, and it feels all too familiar. Home is an unpredictable minefield where fighting can break out on an ordinary afternoon, right after you get home from school or church, and no one expects it to be different or to be protected from it. I didn't even have the language to ask for different or for protection. I do not remember where I drive. I do not know what comes next that day or that evening or the one after that. I know that I bring my little brother home at some point. I do not know if apologies or explanations are offered. I know that I expect neither. And never, not once, do my little brother or I talk about that ride.

* * *

I have never had a concussion, but I imagine it feels like that year, the year my mother died and my father remarried. The year I tell myself never happened. The year of confusion and constantly jumping scenes with no sense of continuity. It is worse than the years my mother was sick because at least then we were allowed to be sad. Now we are not.

There is a megachurch that my father and stepmother are now attending, and there are endless prayer meetings and healing services that I try to avoid. One afternoon, though, I am present when my stepmother begs the pastors to pray for her on behalf of her son. They lay hands on her in one of the church classrooms, and I am sitting on the chair across the aisle. The window is a square of bright light that is everything good and warm and safe that lives outside this room. I sit in the room with her, but I am not with her. I am not really here, I tell myself. This is happening to someone else.

A pastor with curious eyes asks if he can pray over me.

"No, thank you," I tell him.

Now his eyes are surprised, and I can see he wants to insist.

"No," I say again. He can tell I mean it. It is a relief to tell someone no.

* * *

There is a day when my father discovers I have partially re-corded over one of my stepbrother's videotapes. It wasn't intentional. I simply didn't think my program would run long enough to record over some of his. That fact turns out to be the accelerant for my father's blaze.

"It's that you just don't care!" he yells, his hands punctuating his meaning, swinging back and forth in frustration. "You just don't even care about anybody else! You selfish, bloody little shit!"

I'm standing in front of the television with the videotape in my hands. I am completely still, so as not to let the flames leaping and spitting and hissing around me scorch my skin.

"I'm sorry, Dad. Really. I'll fix it."

I have no idea how to fix it.

"You refuse to make them feel welcome in this house. I'm so tired of you. You selfish little shit. That's what you are, you know? So bloody selfish."

I swallow, slowly. I don't break eye contact with my father. I nod. I keep nodding. "I hear you, Dad. I'm sorry. I was wrong. I know how to fix it. Let me go fix it before he gets home."

I walk across the living room that is a bed of hot coals, and my spine feels naked and exposed. But my father lets me pass. I take the tape and my car keys and drive to the house of one of my mom's best friends. There is a weird nugget of memory that has surfaced in my shaken mind, and I remember hearing once about how they have two VCR machines and often make recordings from one to the other. First, I stop by the video store to pick up a copy of the movie I recorded over. I remember holding the hard, oblong plastic case in my hands. The cover poster image was of two girls my age laughing over their shoulders at the camera, both wearing jeans with the butt cut out. I stare at the naked butts of these girls that my father wants my stepbrother to have back. I feel like I'm back in that parking lot in Philadelphia. I take the dirty movie to my mom's old friend in the house where my father first broke the news that my mom had cancer.

I tell my mom's friend about my mistake. She understands from my face how serious it is that I fix it. She is like a small, spry bird; her eyes miss nothing. She is used to decoding the language of teenagers. She simply nods and bobs and hugs me and sets up the machines to rerecord the film with its sexy, violent plotline in its entirety onto the desecrated cassette.

We don't talk about copyright violations. We don't talk about what is happening at our house. We drink tea and make small talk about I don't even know what. But underneath the small words are the big words. I hear what she is saying. I am terrified she will say it out loud. I don't know how to translate my father for her. I see her watching me and hear her saying in her everyday ways, "I love you. I see you. I am not deaf. I am not blind."

I am, though.

I am mute and immobilized.

I am as disoriented and concussed as a field mouse facing off against a cobra.

*   *   *

My father and his best friend used to catch snakes—a hobby of farm boys. They would use a stick similar in shape to a water divining rod, with its forked end and long body, to pin the snake's head to the earth. The cobra can stand almost upright on its tail, the kings as high as a man's waist. Pinning a cobra's tail is as useless as it is dangerous. It's the head that has to be forced to the ground before it can spit or strike at you. The head must be pinioned flat with the forked end of your snake stick, and only then can you pinch that furious hood behind the venom glands, until it is unable to get a fang into your hand or a shot off at your eyes. It's a little like farm-style Russian roulette.

They'd milk the poison into empty jam jars, forcing the cobras to bite into a plastic bag they'd stretched across the top of the jar; the snake would strike the plastic, head held in place, in impotent spasms of fury and poison. Each strike can deliver just about a teaspoon of venom, more than enough to take down all seven tons of an elephant. They caught a cobra once strong enough and long enough to stand waist high. But it was humbled into the confines of an empty extra-long glass fish tank. Being farm kids, they fed their snakes fresh mice they caught themselves. There were no pet stores, no way to order precaught, frozen rodents for their snakes. It was always do-it-yourself.

They brought the great snake a live mouse, dropped into the far end of the glass box. Cobras smell through their tongues; they lick the air and suck up the essence of their prey, tasting, evaluating, tracking before they strike. Fast and unpredictable, cobras rarely have to strike twice, their bodies snapping back as soon as they've delivered the hit.

The mouse was mesmerized by my father's cobra. Eyes wide and frozen, it stood pasted to the side of the glass. Then came the snap of the strike, and the mouse about literally jumped out of its skin, shooting straight up, the cobra's head missing by millimeters and cracking into the hard shell of the glass instead. Boys, cobra, mouse were all stunned. And then the cycle repeated itself: strike, jump, crack. And again: strike, jump, crack. And again: strike, jump, crack. Until the snake was weaving and facing as unlikely a knockout as when Buster Douglas, the 42–1 underdog KO'd then world heavyweight champion Mike Tyson.

Paralyzed by fear until the last second, the mouse leapt up again and again and again until it had about killed my father's cobra. So they released it—the mouse that defeated the snake. Not despite its fear. But because of it.

* * *

I move through our house like a field mouse waiting for the strike. I can feel the skin between my shoulder blades tingling, I am so sure the hit will come. And when it does, it still manages to take me by surprise. I don't jump fast enough.

It is the week I will be baptized. All my friends have already taken this journey of spiritual symbolism. But I have waited, resisted, because I am holding out on giving up ground in small territories in my life and I don't want to be baptized in my father's new church. I don't want to be baptized because I'm a certain age or because everyone else is doing it. I want to wholeheartedly believe in what I am doing.

The whole long, disorienting year I have been carving out a sliver of space for my own thoughts, my own choices, my own faith. It's a love story really. In the midst of raging loss and suspicion of church and elders, healing and hysteria, I find a quiet place, an eye in the center of all that rages around me, and it is Jesus. He is the same Jesus my mom held tight to the night she died. I am not afraid of Him. I am not angry at Him. He is the only thing from my other life that still holds. So I hold on to Him, and I have decided to be baptized in the church my friends and I have adopted, on the other side of town from my father and stepmother's mega-venue.

I go dancing on Saturday nights and I sit in a church pew on Sundays and I sing the doxology at the end of every service and I believe there is a God who is holding my hand and pulling me up out of the water. I take a deep breath and decide it's time. It's my time to lie down in that holy water so that He can pull me up out of it and resuscitate me with His living breath and everyone can know that I am His and He is mine.

My stepmother wants to be invited. She isn't not invited. Everyone is invited. My friends are all coming. My friends from church, from youth group, from clubbing, from school are all coming. My father and brothers are coming. My stepmother wants me to want her to come. She wants me to invite her in person. This is what my father tells me one night in the living room. She is downstairs in the car, and he wants me to go down there and tell her how much I want her to come to my baptism. I don't want her to come. And I don't want to ask her to come. I don't say these words out loud. But he has had nearly two decades of experience interpreting my body language.

I am sitting on the leather sofa across from the TV that is off. My father is pacing in front of me, punctuating his words with a furious index finger. "You need to go down there and invite her. You need to go right now. She's *waiting*."

I hold very, very still. He weaves and paces.

"Listen to me. *Listen* to me; this disobedience is unacceptable. Do you hear? You will not disrespect my wife like this. I won't let you. I won't let you poison our family like this."

I am not moving. I can't move. I don't know how to move. But I don't speak. The quieter I am, the angrier he gets. The room is blurring now. I see the fireplace on the left, Grandpa's prize-winning kudu horns mounted above it and the shrapnel casing of an exploded ordnance he'd brought back from Egypt and had mounted and engraved for Grandma with his own handwriting. I see my reflection in the glass sliding door across from me and feel how cold the tiles are under my feet.

"How dare you ignore me like this? Hey?! I'm talking to you, dammit." And he smacks his palm on the coffee table.

I am staring straight ahead. I don't realize it, but I am a foreshadowing of my own son, how I will teach him to turn to marble in the face of my rage the way I have learned it from my father.

"Look at me. *Look at me!*" he screams, and little flecks of saliva bead the corners of his mouth.

I don't think he will hit me with his hands. But I know that violence comes in all forms. I have gone many rounds with my father's temper. I never win. He will knock me out. I just don't know how yet. I brace against his words that come fast now, like punches. Like strikes. I don't jump. I don't move. I don't reply. I let my body absorb the blows. I don't know any other way. This is our way. This is our family. This is our story.

And then his voice drops to a hiss and our eyes lock as he points his finger directly at me and says, "I despise you, you know that? I spit in your face." He pauses and enunciates each word, including the name of his dead wife: "I. spit. in. your. face. Lisa-Jo."

And there it is. I don't get out of the way in time. It is a fatal hit.

He kicks the couch where I am sitting. And I get up and I go downstairs and I coax my stepmother into coming to my baptism.

* * *

When I come up out of the water, the first thing I see is the sunlight, pouring like golden rain through the clerestory windows of the church. I am dripping water and sunshine as I step out of the baptismal pool. I have given my testimony, I have told my story—my "Jesus loves me, this I know" story—and then I have lain down in the water and let Him raise me up as His beloved daughter with whom He is well pleased. I dry off and change and make my way back to the sea of people who have come to celebrate with me. I love the eclectic mix of friends from all the trails of my life who have converged in this sanctuary where we are all safe and welcome.

My stepmother comes to find me. I am in a pew surrounded by my people and a deep sense of love. It is like a force field around me. I think she senses it. She smiles. She greets my friends. Then she proves all over again that truth is still stranger than fiction as she tells friends who've never stepped foot in a church before, let alone a baptism service, in her sugary high voice, "This isn't our church, though. My husband and I go to a much bigger church where you can really feel God's power working."

Then she smiles as the conversation parts before her and turns to me. "Congratulations, Lisa-Jo. This is for you." She hands me a small white envelope.

I'm surprised. I take it and my mouth forms a smile at her. I feel a weight on my chest try to shift. Like maybe I will be able to start taking real, deep breaths again instead of small, scared ones. I open the card. I read her loopy cursive. My brain struggles to interpret what she has written. It goes something like this:

I'm glad you have given your life to God, Lisa-Jo. I hope you will listen to Him. I hope you will repent for how selfish you have been. I hope you will realize that going to study in America is taking food out of my own child's mouth. I hope you will tell your dad you don't need to take his money, that you are sorry you asked him to spend so much on you. You need to think about my son and what he needs and how there won't be enough left for him if you go study overseas. I hope after today you start to change.

I can still feel the jolt of that strike hitting my body.
I am as surprised as if the envelope itself had bitten me.

* * *

At the end of the year, my father divorces my stepmother. Not because of the note she wrote me. Not because of the black eye her son gave him. Not because of all the money she spends. Not because of their explosive fights. Not because he suspects she is stealing from him. But maybe because he starts to fear for his kids. At least, this is what he tells his pastor.

He is sitting in the small townhouse living room of one of the elders of our church. Our old church. The church my mom and dad attended together. The church where I went to youth group and used to sneak leftover communion bread to play "pretend church" with my friends. The church where we held my mom's memorial service and where my father once told the pastor he was so angry at God for not healing his wife that his words were like a physical force. I had felt them where I was standing—in the long church entranceway with its gray slate tiles and stained glass hallway opening onto a small court-yard. My dad was upstairs in the pastoral offices. But his voice was a living, breathing creature and I had heard it rearing up for the strike and I was hypnotized by it. By hearing what would come next.

Our conservative Afrikaner pastor responded in shocked tones in his heavily accented English, "But you can't be angry at God."

My father had bellowed in reply, "I'm not angry. I'm *furious!*"

I felt the seismic aftershocks of his words run through my body. The empty church seemed to quake and quiver, the walls absorbing the truth screaming down their halls. That was one of the last times we were in my mom's church.

Now we're sitting in the small townhouse because my dad wants to return to his home church, since he can't go back to his actual home. We're there because he has been called to give an account for his divorce in a sect where divorce is a sin greater than domestic violence. I know this because they tell us. One of the elders tells my father that a wife must always submit to her husband, forgive him, and keep offering him her sacrificial love, come what may. In the same way, the risk of physical violence to children is batted away like a gnat.

This is not a homecoming. This is a formal excommunication service.

The pastor and his elders are uncomfortable that I am there.

"Why did you bring Lisa-Jo? This isn't appropriate." They don't make eye contact with me. I am sitting next to my dad. We are in hard, straight-backed chairs, facing a semicircle of white faces and dark beards and glasses and three-piece suits all with wide, thick ties.

"I thought he needed someone with him. To speak on his behalf," I tell them.

They don't acknowledge me. Not with a flick of their eyes or a swivel of their heads.

My dad unfolds his surgeon's hands. They are like a delicate prayer that he holds out before him in supplication to the men sitting in judgment of his faith.

"I'm so sorry. I know that the marriage was a mistake. All I can tell you is that I was out of my mind. You saw me go out of my mind. You know me. And I'm begging you now. I'm begging you to forgive me."

"Listen, we're sorry for what happened to Jo." They shuffle uncomfortably in their seats. "But Scripture is clear. Divorce is not permissible. It is unacceptable. It is just sin. Plain and simple."

The youngest elder's pale skin is flushed, almost aroused. He has been married less than a year. He has no kids and bears no grief yet. His mouth works around the words, and I can tell he likes the taste of them. "We have no place for you or this behavior in our church."

My dad looks down at his hands. "I understand. I understand. All I can do is tell you how sorry I am. And ask you to let us come back."

His vulnerability surprises me. The brevity of this interaction surprises me. I realize we are about to be dismissed. I take a slow, long breath. And then I exhale my womanhood, my voice, my twenty years of growing up inside the Bible stories told by my father, into the room.

"What about grace?" I ask.

Still, no one looks in my direction.

"What about how the Bible talks about forgiveness? What about how we're supposed to love one another as Christ loved us? Don't you think we're supposed to love my dad like that?"

Slow eyes slide my way.

Did you know that a group of vultures is called a committee? But when they are feeding together at a carcass, the group is called a wake.

This is my father's wake.

I see it clearly in their eyes.

We stand up. We leave the room. We leave the church that we are never allowed to return to.

But somehow, neither of us leave the faith or each other.

But now my father is the one who is concussed.

CHAPTER 7

Coming to America

Like my grandfather before him, my father pays for me to go to university. I will fly from Johannesburg back to the American East Coast, where once upon a time my dad got his master's in theology and I graduated kindergarten. I'd grown up on stories from our three years in Philadelphia, and so going to America for college was a very respectable way to run away from home. My grown-up self is surprised to remember that I didn't give my brothers a second thought. I just fled. I left them and my dad and the house still haunted by the specter of an evil stepmother and flew backward through time to finish my education in the country where it had begun.

We stand in line at the ticket counter in Johannesburg, and I am worried. Not about moving halfway across the world by myself. Not about who my roommate will be. Not about culture clash or homesickness. I am worried about a much more practical, a much more terrifying kind of sickness.

"Did you bring the Dramamine?" I ask my dad.

I can tell by his blank face that he did not. Terror claws at my insides. I have spent one too many flights clutching a metal airplane toilet bowl to believe that this kind of unmedicated journey could end any other way.

"Stay here. I'll check the airport pharmacy," he says and dashes off, leaving me with passport and wallet in hand, backpack way too heavy and anticipation now struggling with anxiety.

When he comes back, he is all medical certainty as he opens a small box and takes out two elastic bracelets and slips them onto my wrists.

"What do these do?" I ask him, frowning down at my arms.

"They press down on key pressure points in your wrist," he tells me.

"But where's the medicine?" I ask. "Do they release some kind of medication into the skin?"

"No, just a kind of acupressure that targets your balance centers," he says.

My eyes meet his with disbelief and growing horror.

"What?! I need medicine, Dad. I need strong medicine. I need it directly into my bloodstream."

"This will be fine, you'll see," he says. Neither of us believes him.

That's what I remember about our goodbye. I don't remember being sad. I don't remember him praying for me or any words of encouragement or parental advice he may or may not have offered. I remember those bracelets and the sense of utter uselessness, staring at them. And for the next eleven hours of the flight from Johannesburg to London and the eight after that from London to Boston, I am handcuffed to the toilet bowl. In between bouts of offering up the contents of my stomach to the travel gods, I notice a couple of cute Dutch boys noticing me. But I am green, and my eyes roll back in my head in frustration and exhaustion, and I pray for the trip to end.

America arrives like a nauseous blur, and it takes all my last resolve to fill out the immigration card before the wheels mercifully touch down on solid ground. The sticky August air is like a welcome hug, and I let it carry me slowly through customs and immigration and to baggage claim, where I sit down on my suitcase and wait. A girl arrives holding a sign with my name, and she is less than enthused to meet me. She gathers up one other international student and whips us through the hinterland surrounding Logan Airport, along the winding, weird roads that shoot through strip malls and industrial complexes and quaint neighborhoods to run their way to the coast, hugging the northeastern edge of the world. But it's impossible to see the ocean because of the trees that clutter up the route with their leaves and branches and trunks standing on their tiptoes, blocking out the sky. And this carsick, airsick South African can add horizon sick to her first glimpse of life back on the East Coast.

"This is a seatbelt," the student escort had helpfully told me. I raised an eyebrow and didn't have the energy to explain that since I'd arrived on an airplane it was probably safe to assume that I'd made my acquaintance with seatbelts back in South Africa. Although, to be fair, we're not super keen on them and most of my childhood didn't involve one. This was the first in a long list of sometimes amusing, sometimes frustrating assumptions my American peers would make about my country of origin.

"How far do you have to go to see lions?"

"Have you ever ridden an elephant?"

"Can you use a knife and fork?"

At the top of the list was the constant surprise that I was White. "You're from South Africa? No way! Aren't you supposed to be Black?"

I was never sure how best to respond to such an uneducated assumption. When I touched down on Boston's North Shore in the fall of 1994, our beautiful country with its brutal history had just celebrated its very first democratic election. My first year of college was also the first year that every race in our country was permitted to vote. Wrap your mind around that. Just 14 percent of the population was White like me in 1994. And it was the first time ever that our tiny, iron-fisted minority weren't the only ones at the polls deciding the future of the other 86 percent. The political prisoner and folk hero Nelson Mandela, who had spent twenty-seven years in a cell, became president, apartheid was officially ended, and we had a new constitution, a new national anthem, and a new flag. Hadn't they heard of the downfall of apartheid, the South African cousin of slavery voted into law by people who shared my lack of melanin? Of course South Africa had White people.

But how does a twenty-year-old pack three hundred years of history into less than three hundred words when she's asked the same question what feels like three hundred times? So, eventually I'd shake my head and simply say, "No, not Black. I'm White." And hold up my arms as evidence of the extremely pale truth of that statement while wondering how our Red Sea moment hadn't made news here on the outskirts of the power seat of American politics. But apparently the event that had earthquaked our country hadn't sent its seismic ripples as far as the small Christian liberal arts campus that would be my home for the next four years.

The beautiful school nestled into the North Shore of Massachusetts was a rolling panorama of fall greens and reds and oranges and was also bright white as far as the eye could see. People were kind and curious and endlessly fascinated by the accent I didn't realize I had. If I had told them I was a princess, the daughter of a South African chief or king, they would have believed me. I was a walking curiosity. But I was proud of my country and over and over again repeated the same phrase, "No, I'm not Australian. No, I'm not British. I'm South African." One time when I was on hold with the bank, trying to set up a way for my dad to send me money, a teller asked me, "What country?" when I was giving her my home address.

"South Africa," I replied.

"Yes, what *country?*" she said with an irritated edge to her voice.

"South Africa *is* a country," I explained in surprise.

If I'm honest, I think I liked the attention. It was a way to fit in—by being different, being the foreign student. It became my shtick. It was kind of cool. Like my red lipstick, my crop tops, and my chunky black boots with the high heels, I wore *South African* like a fashion accessory. Until the day I met Grace.

* * *

My dad knew better. We had both landed in America as students in August—two decades apart. While my first thought was, "I wonder if I can make it to campus without throwing up again?" my father's had been, "It feels as hot and humid as Manguzi, Zululand." My father had made good on his non-farming dream and qualified as a doctor of family medicine before he arrived in the States. He'd graduated from the prestigious University of Cape Town, where his baboon-hunting uncle's photograph still hung in the Chief of Surgery's office, then left the big city for the mango groves and traditions of the tribal lands of the Zulu people. KwaZulu, the place of the Zulus, is where my just barely married parents would deliver their firstborn into the world.

My dad had been interning at the remote Methodist hospital as a student during his med school breaks, and after graduation, after his residency under Dr. Christiaan Barnard (the surgical god who plowed his way through all the pigs the pork board would give him en route to perform the world's first human heart transplant), my father drove my heavily pregnant mom in their white VW Beetle stuffed with suitcases, good intentions, and a cat from Stradbroke they'd named Straddles up the north coast from Durban to the foot of the Lebombo Mountains. Then their Beetle crawled its way up the steep, narrow, winding mountain track and back down the other side. They crossed the sandy Makatini Flats, so often underwater in the rainy season, and emerged through the heavily vegetated, almost tropical forest, at Manguzi Mission Hospital.

This tiny outpost of the Methodist Church grew from a seed planted and watered by the despair and prayers of a German prisoner of war, who once promised God that if he ever survived his World War II Russian prison camp, he'd dedicate his life to serving in the most impoverished area in the world. And his mission is still there today and still called Manguzi, named for the groves of mango trees it's surrounded by.

Dad didn't speak much isiZulu in the beginning. When he first met *Nkosi* (Chief) Mzimba Tembe, he needed a translator to negotiate help for the hospital with the sewage system located on the chief's lands. But three years later, by the time I arrived with my parents for the first time in America, I was babbling in isiZulu more than English and would struggle to blend into American culture. I know my parents didn't transplant easily either. They lived in thirteen houses their first year until they finally landed in a home that was permanent enough to deserve the title. I don't know how my mother managed. But then again, she's the same woman who had followed my father into a chapter straight out of *King Solomon's Mines* and bore down and delivered me in a remote rural hospital where the only doctors were my dad with his brand-new medical degree and his former med school classmate and friend, only more experienced by a nose.

When they arrived in mango country in the rainy early days of summer, the dark fog of apartheid was settling low and terrible across South Africa's cities and escarpments. In 1948, the Afrikaner National Party, descended from what was born in Middelburg, had come into power and instituted their policies of apartness—literally translated *apartheid*—for the various races. In 1950 the Population Registration Act classified all South Africans into one of four racial groups: "White" (of European descent), "Coloured" (of mixed ethnic origin), "Indian" (of Indian or Pakistani descent), and "Black" (indigenous people). And in South Africa's racial hierarchy, this dictated access to education, healthcare, employment, and housing. All groups were subservient to White. Black South Africans, suffering the most curtailed rights, "stood at the very bottom of this steep hierarchy" and the Indian and Coloured groups allowed "some employment and mobility privileges denied to black South Africans yet still making them subservient to the white South African population."[1] And by 1970, when my dad was chugging the eighteen-hour drive between medical school and Manguzi, the government was passing the Bantu Homelands Citizenship Act. Millions of indigenous people (Bantus) would be herded into designated Black-only areas (homelands), also known as Bantustans. Think Jim Crow meets Indian reservations for each of South Africa's indigenous people groups.

The Zulu people, who could trace their ancestors to centuries before Europeans set foot in Cape Town, who had been united under the military genius of Shaka, who had waged war on all the surrounding tribes, establishing their dominance in the territory, were dispossessed of their South African citizenship and their privately owned prime real estate in lieu of citizenship in lesser land, the new Bantustan of KwaZulu. This became the place of the Zulus, the birth story of Zululand and the birthplace of a White child who would be named after her mother.

My father once plotted down to the last detail how he would have helped the Zulu army defeat the Boers at the Battle of Blood River. I believe that he believed we loved our Black countrymen. I certainly believed it. But as Scripture says, faith without works is dead. And healthy belief must grow legs that walk out its faith in real time, in practical ways. I think it is easy to become enamored with the legend of Shaka while galloping past the basic needs of the people living in their pocket-square-sized houses on the hill behind your farmhouse.

But after unpacking his car and his wife and his cat, my father did the most radical thing you can do for your faith and your racism—he became friends with flesh-and-blood people. *Baba* (Father) Zondo would take my parents into his story, his language, his shared cooking pot, his community, and his heart. And by the time I was a two-year-old toddling through his door, he would approach the local *InDuna* (leader) on behalf of my parents to seek permission for them to build a house next door to the Zondos—a traditional Zulu house made of stick and mud and plastered over with cement, a drum in the roof for water, and outside the perimeter of the Whites-only compound. The *InDuna* graciously approved and allocated my father a piece of land beside Baba Zondo's home.

Mosquitos swarmed thick and dangerous in Zululand, spreading malaria and fear, like the political informants who buzzed with news of my father's conversation with the *InDuna*. Days later threats and the secret police arrived like smoke blowing in from the cooking fires, stinging the eyes and my parents' plans. In the midst of the clinic's fast-moving daily stream of fifty to seventy physical exams, TB diagnoses, tooth extractions, and maternity checkups, my father returned to his table of files and a cup of tea only to discover an anomaly—another White man.

"Oh, hello," my young father said. "Can I help you?"

"Actually, perhaps I can help you," came the reply, in the thick guttural accent of a Dutch immigrant.

My father says he knew immediately who the man was, with his dirty blond hair greased severely back, dressed in khaki shorts and long brown socks with a comb stuffed down the right-hand leg. This deep in Zululand there were no tourists, no White people outside of the hospital and church staff. Only the secret police ventured this far into the homelands.

"No, I'm fine; there's nothing I can think of I need help with," my father said as he leaned against his desk, long legs casually crossed, arms folded over his white medical coat, stethoscope around his neck.

"Well, don't be so sure," came the smug reply from the man with the deep sunburn sitting comfortably in my dad's small space.

"How can you help me?" my father asked.

"I have strong information that you are of a plan to build a house near the house of Mr. Zondo, outside the complex." The heavily accented statement with its awkward transliteration wound around my father's gut like the *boomslange,* tree snakes, we had to watch out for when playing outside.

"I want to tell you, don't do that. This is the place you must stay, on this compound."

My dad held the eyes of this man as he asked the question they both knew the answer to: "Why shouldn't I leave? It's not that far away."

"It's a Black area; this is the White area."

"How can this be a White area in the middle of KwaZulu? This is a Black Bantustan," my dad said with a slight inflection of amusement.

"Well, this is a White area here in the hospital," came the reply with perfect apartheid logic. "The Blacks who work here are temporary residents in the White area."

"Well then, I can be a temporary resident in a Black area," my father reasoned. The room was quiet enough to hear the nursing sisters down the hall making tea and opening the biscuit tin. There was no air-conditioning. A small table fan was trying to circulate the muggy air, coughing over the impossible task.

"If you try to do that, the house that you are going to build could burn down."

"No." My father tried to shrug the absurd words away. "I'll build it safely."

"No." The man paused, speaking slowly, never breaking eye contact. "I am warning you that it will burn down."

Then he stood up, his shirt sticking to his back, and said over his shoulder, "I came here in friendship to warn you, but it looks like I've wasted my time." And he walked away down the long corridor.

Giant fences surrounded the hospital compound. And my father was aware of the incongruence of preaching a Gospel that commands we love our neighbors as ourselves, while walling ourselves off from our neighbors. Mandela's political party, the African National Congress (ANC), was still an outlawed terrorist group and would not become the governing party for another two decades. And while we might watch ordinary people morph into superheroes in the movies over our popcorn and under cover of darkness and fantasy, real life can leave us squinting awkwardly into the sharp reality that making contact with one of the members of an underground political party is no ninety-minute plotline.

No one my father talked to would admit to being in the ANC, and to keep asking, to keep trying to connect, was to risk the bush telegraph bringing back the secret police with their threats and matchboxes. My dad says he didn't try as hard as maybe he could have; maybe he should have. He didn't want their lives or the lives of their Black friends to catch fire. And he had at his disposal that most exclusive of all privileges: choice. He could choose to leave.

So, in their third year in Zululand, my father started sending applications like ballast from a sinking ship to universities all over the world. He wanted a chance to dissect the intersections of faith and racism they were living in. And he knew firsthand how resistant South African universities were to entertaining conversations at odds with the theology of apartheid. At the same time, he was sending letters to the Department of Native Affairs in Pretoria asking for budget approval for a new labor ward for their hospital. That letter, like Morse code, tapped its way through the crisscrossing red tape, and he received a long-distance phone call in reply.

"No, there's no budget available for that," said the disembodied voice of the apartheid state that had taken over the administration of the hospital.

"But listen, do you know the conditions we're delivering babies in?" My dad tried to reason with the voice. "We're desperate here. Babies are being delivered like outpatient procedures!" My dad was sweating and frustrated and couldn't understand what the voice on the other end wasn't saying.

"This used to be a Methodist mission hospital," my dad tried to explain again. "But since the government has all but taken over operations now, I'm telling you what we need to keep servicing your hospital."

The voice shrugged, saying in its guttural Afrikaans accent from a thousand miles away, "I need to explain something to you, Doctor. You want a maternity ward, yes? Well, what's that going to do for the people, hey? It's going to make more healthy Black babies to be born. The government policy is that we don't want more Black kids. If you want a TB ward or a surgical unit or something else, we'll find the money for it. But if you want a labor ward, it's not going to happen."

My father was accepted to Westminster Theological Seminary in Philadelphia. And so my parents packed up the cat and their three-year-old daughter, her yellow crib, and the sand from the Makatini Flats that now coated the inside of their car. Baba Zondo and his wife were not surprised.

The last thing my father did before he left Manguzi was to submit the plans for a new operating room that the government approved. It would be used as a labor and delivery ward. Then my father and mother scuttled back out from under the mango groves in the Beetle they had arrived in.

My dad tells me the goodbyes physically hurt. I believe him. Baba Zondo is in his nineties now, and he and my father are still friends. The nursing staff had lined the hallways of the hospital, singing their *hamba kahle* (goodbye). The staff, when anonymously polled, had all answered the question "Do you think the White missionary doctors are here because it's where they could find jobs or because they are called by God to love and serve you?" with, I imagine, the number-two-pencil version of a shrug and a check mark next to the box "Because it's where they could find jobs."

I don't think my father saw the binary trap the question set, but I know he believed South Africa was being poisoned by apartheid and was convinced that for his faith to walk out of the pages of the Good Book, he needed to move off the hospital compound and dissociate from whiteness and the mission with its mixed motives. But the secret police had cut that hope off at the legs. And he was convinced that any theology he studied in South Africa would be infected with racism. So they drove away from the Zondos, the Zulu harmonies, my first home, and the naïve belief that simply wanting to make a difference was enough.

My parents would touch down in Philly just a few weeks later. And my dad would get his master of arts in religion and in his third year research and write a thesis for his master of divinity on "The Afrikaner Covenant." Like his daughter would twenty years later, he came to America to dismantle the toxic theology of his childhood.

* * *

Grace was in the college Gospel Choir with me. Or maybe it would be more accurate to say that I was in the Gospel Choir with Grace. Her voice was like an oak tree—strong, powerful, offering shelter to others who were too shy or too nervous to sing in public, like me. But we met way before we were in choir together. We met out in the center of the green quad between the dorm buildings and the library. It was a late summer afternoon, and I was in that freshman phase where you're still constantly meeting new people. We both stood out. Me because I was South African, she because she wasn't White on an almost all-White campus. Her brown hand was in my white one, and I was halfway through my introduction before I noticed that her face had gone quiet, blank. Brown eyes staring out of a brown face. And then I was already being introduced to someone else and we all kept walking.

It would be after choir, after our first concert, after the leaves had all died dramatically in shades of violent red and we'd been friends for a semester that Grace would tell me what she was thinking that first time we shook hands: "I couldn't believe I was touching the hand of a White South African."

I got very still. I wasn't sure what to say. Grace knew. She knew the horrors of apartheid and had been horrified to be hand in hand with a White South African. She wasn't surprised that I was White. She was surprised that she could become friends with me.

"His eye is on the sparrow, and I know He watches me," she once sang in a fierce solo on stage. And my eye was on Grace because I knew that she knew. She knew the shadows cast by my whiteness. Becoming my friend was an act of faith and trust I don't think I was equipped to fully understand at the time. Her name became her gift to me, and I knew her friendship wasn't lightly given. I tried to hold it in both my hands.

*   *   *

My mom had been pregnant when my parents landed in the States, and my brother would be born three days after their first Christmas in America. And two years later, when the world had spun forward to summer, he would accidentally slam our thick wooden front door on my small hand. I screamed and screamed and was unable to wrench the door handle around with my left hand to free myself because my right was trapped in the mechanism. When my dad forced that door open, my entire fingernail came with it.

At the ER the doctor couldn't understand my sobbing in broken English and isiZulu and my fear of the dreaded *umjovo*.

"What's she saying?" he asked my dad.

"She's scared of getting an injection," my dad replied while swaddling the blood-soaked bath towel around my hand.

"What's an injection?" I whispered from dry lips.

"An *umjovo*," my dad whispered back as he wiped hair and sweat out of my eyes.

My baby brother would toddle up to me with snacks and a juice box from the vending machine as a peace offering. That door, that pain, that ER room, that injection, those stitches, that snack—those would be the first memories that are my own and not handed down from someone else's stories.

I wonder if that memory is the reason I think of my father as a doctor almost before I think of him as a dad. He spoke medicine like he spoke isiZulu—in a way that made him an almost mythical character in my mind. His presence in an emergency room or an emergency is like gravity. He pulls you down, centers you with his authority, his focus, his knowledge of what is happening. And even as a wounded five-year-old, I recognized that my father was translating, explaining the pain. He has always been my favorite teacher about anything to do with the body. He can explain almost any physical hurt you bring to him. His reputation as a diagnostician is legendary in medical circles. In our family, if you or your kids are sick, if you have cut your head open on the trampoline, if you have a diagnosis you can't make sense of, Dad will come, Dad will fix you, Dad will make it make sense. I had faith in this. It was the assurance of things seen.

I wasn't the only one. He believed this truth too. Like Superman's kryptonite or Achilles's heel, my dad's certainty that he had the training and the skill to diagnose and make you better would be his undoing when my mom got sicker than he could fix. And in the aftermath of her death and his remarriage, it would be the soul wounds of his kids—their broken safety, their bleeding loneliness, their parenting PTSD—that he would misdiagnose altogether.

* * *

Two decades before I arrived in Boston for college, my young mom and dad would both touch down there for a weekend. Dad had been invited to a missions event to talk about the medicine and the faith he practiced in South Africa. On the last night, their host told his congregation, "I want each person to write your name on a piece of paper. Then fold it up."

Then all the scraps were gathered into baskets, like those leftover bits and pieces of fish and loaves from the Bible story, and hundreds of names were shaken up like precious leftovers and then passed back out.

"Now reach into the basket and pick a piece of paper. You're picking a name that God is asking you to pray for."

My dad tells how he imagined getting the name of someone important, some saint from a far-flung corner of the world with a big story that would become part of my father's story as he prayed the way he practiced medicine—deliberately, with zero expectation of failure.

Slowly the baskets made their way back down the aisle to where my mom and dad were sitting. And my father reached a confident hand with its powerful sinews into the confetti of names and drew one out. One singular collection of syllables in that sea of paper. Then the basket passed on and he slowly unfolded the scrap, his lean fingers gently pulling on the creases until he could make out the name. Would it be a foreign name? A missionary like he had been? A name he could cherish and commit to reminding God of every day, as diligently as any doctor scrubs their hands, rinse and repeat and rinse and repeat? He was as focused on that paper as on any operating table he'd stood over when the name came into sight.

He blinked.

Out of an ocean of names he'd stretched out his rod and the one he'd reeled in was the name of the woman sitting next to him. The mother of his children. The name more familiar to him than his own, his wife: Jo.

"I was so disappointed," he would tell me years later. "I felt cheated. I couldn't believe it. Of all the interesting, exciting, or miraculous names I could have got, I ended up with just my wife's!"

He said he balled it up in his pocket. He was embarrassed by the preacher man's belief that God was going to send each individual in that church a significant name, a name intended just for them; he said it felt like a total bust. My mom's name ended up in the scraps and litter and leftovers of the evening after my dad took her home and promptly pushed the exercise out of his head. Years after she lost her battle with leukemia, he would tell me that story. Sitting next to him, I watched as he remembered that night, his elegant hands, with their age spots, folding and unfolding over and over again as if to smooth out a phantom scrap of paper and that name that had slipped from his fingers.

* * *

Two decades later I would land with her name back on American soil. And history would repeat itself. I'd make my way to a campus I'd never visited before, determined to make sense of my country's story. I arrived with my mom's name and my suitcase and opened the heavy front door of Wood Hall. And made my way to the third floor.

There were two tiny dormer windows and three beds; I was the first to arrive. The room was hot and sweaty with the breath of late August. It was my birthday. The girl from Zululand had arrived back in America on the day of her birth. The room was completely empty, except for a bouquet of flowers. I could hear voices yelling hellos across the quad, hear music drifting in the window, and see sunlight settling like a halo around the buds. I dropped the suitcase and backpack and walked over to the flowers. There was a card with my name. With my mother's name.

Dear Lisa-Jo,
Happy birthday, my darling. I love you.

And then he'd had the florist write down a Bible verse: Jeremiah 29:11. I held the small white card in my hands and read my father's words:

"For I know the plans I have for you," declares the Lord,
"plans to prosper you and not to harm you,
plans to give you hope and a future."

CHAPTER 8

Roll Down Your Window

I will marry a man with my father's first name and his exact opposite personality. I don't know that this will be the plan when I leave Boston in the spring of my sophomore year to spend a semester off campus studying in Washington, D.C., where I will meet my Peter. He also speaks fluent faith but comes with an American footballer's hands. They are the kind of hands that no matter how disorienting your day, you believe those hands can catch you and anchor you to the promise that Bob Marley set to music in "No Woman, No Cry," when he sang, "Everything's gonna be alright."

I arrive in D.C. to spend a semester trying to decode what justice means. Like my father before me, I've grown up breathing the toxic air of apartheid, and an urgency to make things right drums in my veins. But I'm uneducated. I know the very barest narrative of the writers, lawyers, artists, and freedom fighters who disassembled the apartheid factory. Instead, I had watched from a fog within the smog, a daughter of White privilege and teenage pain who ran away before she ever clearly saw the world beyond her bedroom window. I knew only the faintest outlines of those who stayed and made history. The kind that isn't romantic. The kind that is exhausting, that hurts, that comes with a very high price tag I have never paid myself.

I found myself like one of our Dorper sheep on dosing day, herded into a crush of confusion and hope, ignorance and escape, directly into the footsteps of the father I am both following and fleeing. Once again, I've traipsed across time zones and continents and my flights have been delayed so many times I put a call through to the D.C. residence director from my final layover to let him know how late I'm going to be.

By the time I land and get my luggage and catch a cab and finally am deposited on Capitol Hill in front of the student row house where I'll be living for a semester, part of the man-made honeycomb that links people street by street, block by block throughout the city, I smell of travel and have been awake for nearly forty-eight hours. I step into the cold January slush of D Street as a group of male students explodes like a pack of noise from the building and scoops me and my suitcase up with shouts of "Hey, the last one is here!"

"You made it!"

"Guess the South African finally arrived."

I don't know that my Peter is there. His first memory of me will be of a girl who looks like a scrap of paper that's been balled up, like a gum wrapper or discarded ticket stub. I don't know that he will become my best friend. And that I will become addicted to hearing his opinions.

A native of Michigan, he has never been overseas. But in the next five months he is quick to learn more about my homeland than I have at my fingertips—population size, demographics, our long walk to freedom, trending music. And in a city celebrated for its museums and monuments, his mind becomes my favorite place to visit. The new Fugees album, theologian Stanley Hauerwas, DC Talk lyrics, baseball, lemon squares, being a pastor's kid, predestination versus free will, LL Cool J—there is nothing I don't want to hear him talk about.

One day in class I pass him a note that must travel across every desk and through irritated hands all the way from one end of the room to the other to reach him. When it arrives at his elbow, I watch him unfold the tiny paper with his big hands. All it says is, "I just wanted to see if I could get this all the way across the classroom." He flicks his green eyes in my direction. I am addicted to getting his attention. He is the straight-A professor favorite. I challenge everything. He smells like Polo Sport cologne and always lingers at dinner so that I have someone to sit with when I inevitably arrive late, rushed, and high from the intensity of my day in a city I am falling in love with. He watches me eat and listens as I tell him the details of my work.

He is endlessly fascinated by my story, and so I start to bring him my highs and lows from my internship at the Office of the District of Columbia Attorney General's Child Protection Section. I am formed by that work. And Peter becomes the safe place to decode what I am seeing, what I am trying to learn. He is unexpected. He says things like, "I heard you and I are the only ones who got an A on that research paper. Can I see yours?"

I think it's a weird thing to ask. "Like, now?" I say as a group of us are hanging out in the student lounge. "It's upstairs in my room."

"Okay, let's go get it." He's shimmering with curious energy and has thick dark hair with a curl that falls across his forehead that I'd like to touch.

I sigh, get up, jog up the stairs ahead of him. We go into my apartment on the top floor and I find the paper, pass it to him. He sits down at the dining room table with my assignment that has a bright red A at the top of it. He has a Bic pen that he spins around in one hand as he reads. I don't know what to do with myself. I fiddle with the dishes in the drying rack, putting them slowly away. And then I notice he's making notes on my paper. I put down a pot and move closer and look over his shoulder.

"What are you doing?" My incredulity is growing.

"Just fixing a few things," comes the reply.

My eyes grow three sizes. "You're doing *what?*"

"No, I mean, it's a good paper. You just have some issues with your grammar in a few places." He's wearing a light blue dress shirt with the sleeves rolled up to his biceps. I can see his right arm flex through the fabric as he deliberately marks up places in my perfect paper.

"You need to go," I tell him.

He doesn't even look up.

"Like now. Dude, just get out." I cannot believe he is correcting something I already got an A for.

He looks up, genuinely confused. "Why?"

"Out. Now!"

He leaves, and I pace and fume and stare daggers at his handwriting in the margins of the lovely lines of my essay. I'm furious and also—I can't help it—fascinated. He is the first man I've met who isn't intimidated by a good intellectual rumble. He nerds out on sentence structure and grammar, and his old high school football T-shirt reads, "Bench Press, 225 Club." He makes ideas sexy.

I'm rolling my paper around in my hands and his impertinence in my mind when the phone rings. "Hey, I made lemon squares. Do you wanna come down and get some?"

I'm still twisting my rolled-up paper around and around in my hands. "What?"

"Lemon squares. They're still hot. Come down."

He has moved on from my insistence on taking offense. Now he wants to feed me. It's addictive, all of it.

* * *

The very first day of my internship we serve a subpoena. I am in the back seat of a small VW Golf. Heather, the staff attorney I've been assigned to, is in the driver's seat. Her paralegal, Patrice, is walking toward a housing project. I have no idea what's going on. I was supposed to be working in a private one-woman firm that dealt almost exclusively with divorce cases. I'd walked out of that office with its lilac shag carpet and soul-crushingly boring interview, across the street in search of a pay phone. I'd found one just inside a parking garage. There was a small puddle of greasy water that had pooled at the base of the pillar the call box was attached to. I straddled the puddle in my brand-new charcoal-gray pumps, one on either side, as I placed a collect call to my dad.

It was after ten P.M. in South Africa. He'd answered and immediately accepted the charges. I started to panic and cry as I choked on my disappointment. "Dad, it's ridiculous. I can't believe this is the internship I got! I'm going to spend all semester stuck in a closet doing research and drafting memos on division of assets between bitter couples. I'm never going to see the inside of a courtroom. This can't be it. This just can't be why I'm here!"

One heel teetered and slipped toward the puddle.

"Ugh, and I'm standing in a freaking pool of grease water under this phone. I can't believe I came all the way for this."

I could hear him catching up quickly, shaking off fatigue as his reply traveled down the line and into my ear. "Then find something else!"

It's always been like that. When he's not against me, his belief in me is fervent, passionate, and catching. And from eight thousand miles away he prayed with the faith of an Old Testament prophet: "Lord, please lead Lisa-Jo to the work you have waiting for her. Please open her eyes and part the seas in front of her."

My dad's larger-than-life voice and vision blew a path through my puddle, my doubt, my Red Sea, and when I got back to my apartment, I started to systematically work my way through the government phone directory, department by department, call after call, to see who was still hiring for the semester. The D.C. attorney general's office was called the Office of the Corporation Counsel at that time, and their chief of the Family Services Division invited me to interview as a legal intern in their Child Abuse and Domestic Violence Section. So my résumé, my pumps, and my new pantsuit made our way to the Judiciary Square metro stop for an interview and orientation. Then on my first official day I don't even have a desk before I'm in the back seat of Heather's car. We watch Patrice knock at the gate of a concrete and brick building. We can't see who opens the door. But we see Patrice pause. Ask a question. Listen. And then shove the papers into the hands of the tenant before hauling her short, curvy self at a surprisingly swift pace straight back to us.

Heather is already putting the car in gear as Patrice pulls open the front door and swings into the passenger seat.

"I told them I was from Washington Gas." She's hanging on to the ceiling handle as the car swings around the corner, and they're ducking and laughing in an explosion of adrenaline. "I stuffed the subpoena into her hands as soon as she confirmed her name."

The car is bumping over D.C.'s notorious potholes as the two women, one short and brown and one short and white, both let out relief and laughter before they remember me and swing amused faces in my stunned direction.

"We don't usually deliver subpoenas ourselves," Heather explains over her shoulder.

Patrice chuckles. "Yeah, but we're pretty good at it when we do!"

It turns out sometimes the police can't track down the witnesses needed in court. And these women spend their days digging out from under the stack of child abuse reports that arrive every morning with the sun and their first cups of coffee. A wire inbox holds the wad of innocuous looking manila files compiled by cops on duty the night before, with their daunting photos and their recommendations, and the attorneys have until two P.M. to prepare petitions to be presented in family court for the removal of minors in danger.

It's a race of words and arguments and keystrokes they repeat every day in and out again. They adopt me as their shadow. I learn the forms, the defense attorneys, the *guardians ad litem,* the chambers that are closed to the public when a minor's case is being heard. I review photos and folders and learn to draft petitions. I try not to have nightmares about belts and bruises and children choked by their parents. Patrice and I sit behind Heather in court and pass up the files she needs when she needs them. The days become a stream of boys' and girls' faces, their paperwork telling stories of D.C.'s then-nationwide lead in child abuse statistics.

* * *

By April the frosted tree limbs lining the streets of Capitol Hill have melted into cherry blossom showers. And I am counting down my last weeks as a student intern and applying for a paid position that will keep me on through the summer. A small group of us are hoping to extend our time in the capital, and Peter already has his think tank gig confirmed. I am still waiting to hear.

On a slow, lazy haze of a Saturday afternoon he drops by my apartment, settles into the corner of the sofa, and, as always, says something totally unexpected. "So, I was talking to God about you."

I turn to face him. "Oh yeah?"

He grins. Unlike most of the guys I know, he is as deeply comfortable in his faith as he is in his skin. He never tries to camouflage his thought process. "Yeah, I was like, 'So, God, I've been thinking about Lisa-Jo a lot lately.' And God was like, 'Yeah, I *know*.'"

I can't stop a snort of laughter. I'm very interested in where this conversation is going. He's watching me watching him as he talks. He likes that he has my full attention. "I told Him, 'Listen, God, if Lisa-Jo doesn't get a job this summer and I never get to see her again, I'm always going to be grateful I met her.'" He lets that sink in.

I can hear the sounds of the city slipping through the open window: kids playing, a jackhammer down below, students calling to each other as they walk to 7-Eleven.

"But," and here is where his eyes drop three shades darker as he holds my gaze, "if You help her get that internship and she stays, Lord, I promise I'm going to be the best friend she's ever had."

I feel that sentence in my stomach.

A week later I'm walking down D Street through Senate Park, passing Union Station on the right and the U.S. Capitol on the left, and I'm caught in a blush and bashful pink shower of cherry blossom petals. The air is cotton candy as spring falls from the sky, and it feels like I'm walking through somebody else's movie. The morning is too sweet, the trees too tender, the breeze too warm, and the landmarks too close to be real.

Growing up, America was *Back to the Future* and *Dirty Dancing* and *The A-Team*. It was all the brands that sanctions kept out of our country: Nike and Levi's and Calvin Klein. America was the Big Mac I'd never tasted until I touched down on the East Coast of the Northern Hemisphere. It was the Golden Arches and the Washington Monument and Paul Simon, who both hijacked and highlighted our music. So, when Peter played his *Graceland* CD and I heard Ladysmith Black Mambazo's Zulu voices rise up over Capitol Hill, singing "Homeless," my heart climbed up out of my chest and lodged itself in my throat. I was a legal alien who'd stepped into a movie and discovered real life. But I was also the child who learned to ululate on the east coast of South Africa and whose mother had played Joseph Shabalala's Zulu funk record on repeat from September 1986 when it came out, crackling with explosive creativity and criticism, to September six years later when she left me motherless and homeless.

And then on the day D.C.'s cherry blossoms serenade me, so soft and sensual, as they fall breathless in my path—that is the day I know I am going to marry Peter Baker. I arrive at work and my blood is acting drunk, hollering in my ears as I hide in an empty office and call one of my roommates and say it out loud: "I'm going to marry Peter Baker. I just know it. I'm freaking out. What do I do?"

And she is just as surprised as I am. "Wait, are you guys even dating?"

"No! He's not even my type. He's too short, he's not blond, he's American. *Ohmywordwhatishappeningtome?*"

I am twenty-one, living in the most powerful city in the world, with only a suitcase and a backpack to my name and the gut instinct that I can actually hear my future grinding slowly in a different direction. I didn't know then that one day our three kids would walk through a cherry blossom spring snowstorm too. I didn't know that one day our sons would spend the night in the apartment that used to be mine when their dad, who grew up to be the director of that same off-campus program, filled in for the residence director one night. I didn't know that the National Mall, where Peter and I once played sunset baseball with our classmates and took the long way home, pausing at the Capitol to watch the skyline change colors, would become the scene of twelve years of class picnics with his students and our young family.

I hang up the phone and my blood is still buzzed when the chief of the Child Support Division tells me they've found a spot for me to work for the summer. I will spend the hottest months in the city talking about sex to a long line of women petitioning for child support. As a twenty-one-year-old White girl with a foreign accent, I will have the job of combing through diaries and calendars with women of all ages and shades to deep-dive when they might have become pregnant so we can make their one-night stands, their drive-by boyfriends, their ex-husbands pay for the babies they were left raising alone.

*   *   *

July in Washington, D.C., is a hellfire of humidity. Peter and I were both broke all the time that summer. I packed a peanut butter and jelly sandwich on white bread and a can of Coke five days a week for lunch. Sometimes I'd go into CVS—the pharmacy with its smorgasbord of beauty products and shelves of snacks—on my lunch break just because of how divine it was to step out of the sauna and into the blessed frozen air. I still quote the old fella who walked in one day looking like a stick of beef jerky wearing a shredded baseball cap and announced to the room, "Damn! It's hotter 'en a witch's tit out there!"

Every afternoon I'd wait outside the office building where I worked in Judiciary Square and watch the escalator that belched up steam and commuters from its belly deep under the city. I would stand and watch, waiting for the dark head of hair to emerge, followed by the steel rims framing the face of the boy I was falling in love with. I could make him smile from across the street. He still smelled like Polo Sport.

He'd be reaching for me before his grin could turn into words, and I'd let him pull me toward him, into him, my eyes exactly level with his, reading the green and the thoughts behind them of what he couldn't do to me in public. My smile would press up against his, my lips politely aware of the lawyers exiting the building behind us. But his hands on my back were a promise. I still wore my charcoal-eyeliner-gray high heels when I really should have known better and switched into sneakers like all the other tired commuters did once it hit six P.M. and they walked home. But he liked my long legs and I liked that he liked them.

We would walk as storybook lovers always have, arms intertwined, taking the long way, spending too much time thinking about how the other person looked, smelled, felt. He was my favorite stalker. He would bat away the obscene propositions that were often flung over backyard fences in my direction as we walked home through neighborhoods that cabbies and coworkers told us would have been safer to drive through. But for that one summer North Capitol Street running in the direction away from power and into the projects was my zip code and this American Peter was becoming my home.

*   *   *

Two girlfriends who had also landed summer jobs join me in that apartment. Peter is the one who found the place we three girls could afford that was still central enough in the city for us to walk to work. When we sign Mr. Gupta's lease, I don't realize that I'm about to step into the tale of two cities—Washington versus D.C. *Washington* rides the metro and commutes in from the suburbs of Maryland and Virginia. *D.C.* rides the bus and lives in the parts of the city that haven't been gentrified yet. *Washington* are the attorneys I work with. *D.C.* are the paralegals and the clients we serve. *Washington* ebbs and flows with the political terms. *D.C.* is local and permanent. *Washington* is primarily White. *D.C.* is primarily Black and Brown. I will learn more about race in one summer in Washington, D.C., than I learned in twenty-one years in South Africa.

The apartment building we move into is across the road from a large housing project. I don't realize that at the time. I'm thinking only about the boy who found us an affordable place to live and how I can feel the heat radiating off his tight T-shirt on the night he helps us move in. There is a group of teenagers hanging out around the front of the building as we carry boxes of pots and pans, suitcases, and a beanbag chair up the steps. I smile at them, nod, acknowledging we are now neighbors. But my smile trips when all we get in return are hard stares. And then my stomach churns when the words slip in behind us before the front door swings closed: "No no no *no,* this is a *Black* building."

I've grown up in South Africa, where my ancestors were the tiniest drop of White in a sea of Black tribes and languages, but, like beachfront property in Cape Town, the right to vote, or access to the best universities, I've had the exclusive luxury of never having to give my skin color any thought at all. Beyond wishing tanning turned my legs golden bronze like my friends, instead of bright red, I had only one memory up until then of actively having to think about the color of my skin.

The summer before I left for college and the long trek to law school in the States, my father suggested I spend the day with one of his patients, a lawyer in the middle of a criminal trial. At the time, apartheid was taking its last gasps and my dad was one of the few White doctors who hadn't abandoned the city center for the suburbs. He had declined the invitation to remain in America to practice medicine and, after three years at seminary spent trying to decode the religion of apartheid, had returned to South Africa in the early eighties convinced they weren't called to abandon ship and bought into a medical practice in Pretoria, the capital city.

Back then White political paranoia was reaching fever pitch, Black exiled leaders of the ANC were being hunted in neighboring countries, and a state of emergency was imminent. In January 1981, only nine days after President Reagan's inauguration and one year after my parents returned to the Southern Hemisphere, South African security forces raided an ordinary suburb of Maputo, the capital of neighboring Mozambique, hitting the houses it thought the banned African National Congress was operating out of.[1] Pretoria had become a powder keg, and White doctors did not treat Black patients.

Except that my dad did.

He told me how one morning his receptionist called him to the front desk because a White patient insisted he be informed that there was a Black person sitting in the waiting room.

"Yes, I know, thank you."

"But, Doctor," the auntie said in shock as she put the pieces together, "you can't see Black patients!"

"Sure, I can," came his reply. "It's right there in the appointment book. Look."

He never saw her again. Not that day and not in the future. And with the other White flight out of the city went many of his patients. But because of his choices in the eighties to keep his doors open to anyone who needed a doctor, by the nineties the former freedom fighters who were then taking up positions in Parliament were also among his patients.

So when he sent me to spend the day shadowing a lawyer, it wasn't just any lawyer; it was a man rising in prominence in political circles.

He picked me up from my dad's practice, where I was sitting in the waiting room. He was a head taller even than my father. He was solid bulk, a Zulu attorney who was comfortable in almost all our twelve national languages. Gerry Jabulani was wearing a navy suit and a crisp white dress shirt. He had a gold ring on his pinky finger and a laugh that was deep and was deeply comfortable in his skin. And in the underground parking lot he had a big, shiny Mercedes-Benz.

It was a three-hour drive to the small town where the trial was taking place. The coffee-colored leather seats were warm from the sun, and Gerry's laughter squeezed into the front seat with his long legs and long arms and big mind that felt like a force field in the small space. As we traveled from Pretoria up past Johannesburg, Gerry cut through Soweto, the Black township that hugs the southern gold-mining belt around the city. Created in the 1930s when the government was trying to sift Black from White, like rock from gold, its name was pulled from the syllabic acronym for Southwestern Townships. Soweto became the largest Black city in South Africa, but until 1976 its massive population serving as domestic workers, nannies, gardeners, and gold miners in Johannesburg couldn't get more than temporary resident status in their country of origin.

I had never been in Soweto. I knew almost nothing about it. Gerry's car groaned over dirt roads that had become rutted by rain and erosion. Kids grinned outside my window, which he rolled down, leaning across the armrest between us and pointing at the faces and bars and corrugated iron roof shanty homes we were cruising past.

"Look!" he boomed. "Look what you have done to my people!"

His index finger was jabbing in accusation, wagging in front of my face, pointing out my window. I was watching a world I'd seen only in news reports slip past my eyes as I felt his frustration, his laughter that was no longer funny. But I didn't understand what he wanted from me. I was a twenty-year-old mute and he was a frustrated tour guide to a world I didn't have language for. I was clueless. I was a child who had been groomed to say and do the right thing. But I didn't know what the right thing was in that moment. *Do I apologize? Do I sympathize? Do I agree?*

"See, see what your people have done to my people!"

I stayed silent. I nodded. I did what he said. I kept my eyes open. Dust was coming in through the window, and I swallowed and looked and tried to see what he wanted me to see. I knew I was not seeing enough.

Then he laughed again, rolled up the window, and rolled back his arm. That was the first time I remember being made aware that I was White. And that my whiteness meant something beyond its literal color.

Until the night we moved into a cheap apartment building across from the projects in D.C.

* * *

Most mornings when I walk to work, there is a proposition waiting to accompany me. He is usually still slurring from the night before, and I try to shrug him off, laugh him off, put him off, but he is always persistent. "Hey, girl, how you doin' today?" he asks as I click-clack down his sidewalk in my lawyer heels. The sun is already threatening to stick my shirt to my armpits.

"Good, I'm good today, thanks."

He weaves into my path, but I keep my eyes ahead. His shadow follows, persists, "Girl, you so fine. I'll get with you, girl. I'll get with a White girl. I ain't no racist."

"Nope." I keep walking as he keeps up. And I stretch the truth. "I'm engaged."

"Nah," he says, keeping pace with me. "I don't see no ring on your finger. And engaged ain't married. I'd still get with you."

I laugh him off. I keep walking like I mean business. And he eventually gives up at the corner, where we part ways.

Most afternoons when I walk home from work, there is another flurry of propositions thrown over chain-link fences in my direction. So Peter always walks with me. His presence dilutes some of the offers, the whistles, the eyes that track my progress through the neighborhood. And I understand that what comes my way is not because I am White. It is because I am a woman. I know this because I am spending every day hearing stories exactly like mine from the Black and Brown women I meet with in my tiny cubicle with its sign tacked to the outside that reads Legal Intern, Child Support Division.

We sit together in the space that isn't meant for two, and I ask quiet questions like, "Can you remember the last time you guys had sex?"

And calendars are discreetly pulled out of handbags, and we scan the pages and the dates together, looking for a telltale star or cross or check mark that we can connect back to the man who once propositioned her across a backyard fence too.

Some of the stories are as colorful as the women who tell them to me. When I ask Rita if she kept a record of her sex life, or the man she thinks is the father, she throws her head back and roars, "Girl! How'm I supposed to remember? That house party lasted three days!"

I try to explain that without a name or dates we can't petition for child support. This is how my days go. And outside the heat is always waiting.

Across the street from our offices is the courthouse, and behind the family services courtroom is a labyrinth of claustrophobic rooms where paralegals hold interviews with the dads who have been summoned to child support hearings. In my first week of the summer, I'm handed a stack of files and told to go find the dad who is named at the top of the petition and see what I can get him to agree to pay. These agreements are then given to the attorney on duty, who stands before the judge with a massive stack of files, which she will present for official approval before the court order is entered. But it is the paralegals in the bowels of the courthouse who do all the heavy lifting.

I walk into my first child support meeting with my file, the child support guidelines, and a calculator and find the dad waiting for me, pacing back and forth in short staccato turns.

"Good morning," I introduce myself. Sit down. Open his file. But before I can begin the calculations, he has both hands on the table, looming over me, and his voice is a crescendo of frustration and indignance. "Listen, I ain't payin' nuthin. You hear me?"

He's wearing slouchy jeans and a baggy sweatshirt, his gold chains vibrating with his voice. "That bitch is bleeding me dry. I'm not paying her another cent! Nuthin,' you hear me, nuthin'!"

And to punctuate that last word he bends down low across the table, and as he hisses the last syllable, spit flies with the sound and I feel it land on my face. I'm stunned still, and then Monique strides into the room and I feel her hand on my shoulder. A veteran paralegal whose slight height is more than a match for the man towering over both of us, she points her commanding finger at his chest and says, "Sir, you need to sit down right now. Right. Now."

He hesitates. But he recognizes the authority she wears and slowly pulls out a chair and sits.

I watch and learn. She sits down next to me, flicks her eyes from his file to his clothes, and explains to him the child support calculator. And as he takes a deep breath to bawl her out, she interrupts, "Those the new Nikes you wearing?"

He's distracted. Surprised. Glances down at his feet. She presses on, "And how much those chains cost you? Huh?"

He looks down at his outfit, confusion written on his face.

"If you can afford those shoes and those chains, you sure can afford another fifty dollars a month for your own child!"

She's filling out the child support order that the attorney will present and the judge will sign off on an hour later.

He's hunched over his hands. He grunts. He signs. And when he leaves, she turns to me and downloads her wisdom and experience: "You gotta remember, you're in charge here. You can't let defendants talk to you like that."

I nod, but I know I'm like a naïve child in here. I can tell she knows that too, but she's simply putting me in the way of learning. And so I learn by seeing and doing.

A week or so later Peter and I will walk to our neighborhood Domino's to pick up pizza for dinner and I'll spot that

man slinging dough behind the cash register. And I'll hide outside, too awkward to face him again in the place where he is
working for the woman he believes is bleeding him dry.

* * *

Pete keeps my fridge stocked all summer and my heart well
fed. He drops by often with groceries he picks up from our
local IGA. At checkout one day a small boy can't quit staring at
him. And like children have always done, he embarrasses his
mother by blurting out what everyone else is thinking: "Mama,
what's a White man doing in here?"

Pete's living across town in a room rented from a local
church. But my apartment is his home base. My apartment,
my neck, my waist. He brings me cartons of chocolate ice
cream and slow, melting kisses. He meets my neighbors.

The first week the girls and I moved in, the guys from upstairs offered us free cable. I thought they meant sharing a pass-
word or account or something. Instead, they meant it literally.
They spliced a cable for us, ran it through the hinge around our
front door, connected it to our TV, and hijacked all the chan-
nels for our viewing pleasure. And later they or their friends or
maybe someone else from the building altogether slipped a
note under the door asking if we'd ever tried brown sugar.

Our building is the left-hand side of a horseshoe with a
parking lot in the center and one tree, like a curious lookout,
on the corner. Its shade is a gathering place for senior members of the community, and one afternoon as Pete and I arrive
back from work, his messenger bag slung across his torso, his
hand planted like a flag in my hand, the group waves at us to
join them under the tree.

"Hey, come over here, you two. Come and meet your neighbors!"

We cross the street to the tree and are surrounded by our elders, and they introduce themselves and, like grandparents all over the world have always done, immediately begin to interrogate us. They already know much more of our business than we could have imagined.

"We heard your garbage disposal was out. Did you get it fixed yet?"

"How long you all been together?"

"We see you coming over till real late every night." This one addressed to Pete.

"We see you walking to work every day. Where you working at?" This to me.

We are introduced to Mr. Dixon, the head of the neighborhood association. He is tall, like my dad. Tall and stately and he gives us his number. Tells us not to hesitate to call if we need help with anything.

We answer all the questions. And my eyes open a bit wider; I see a bit more. I'm not just renting a cheap apartment. I am living inside a community story. While I might live this summer like the huff and puff of a dandelion seed, spinning aimlessly without thought for the whys and hows of the rent I am paying or the building I am living in, this is a community with deep roots and a deeper story, and again, I am the tourist. I shake Mr. Dixon's brown hand and recognize in him a reflection of my father. He is a man not to be trifled with. But he will also have my back.

As we turn to go, one of the women puts what I am feeling into words. "Child," she says, and I look down into her sharp, warm eyes as she sits on her lawn chair, missing nothing about me, "we're watching over you." And as we walk away, my heart feels something familiar, like the opening of a door, the sense of welcome where you don't actually belong, that feels like grace.

After that meeting the morning propositions don't completely stop, but they slow down. The lowriders parked under my window, blasting music and insinuations at two A.M., don't come back. The fire alarm set off outside our door doesn't get pulled again after I call Mr. Dixon and he comes over at midnight to silence it. Then he stands in our living room and I see our story through his eyes, but he opens his arms and hugs me tight like I'm nine and still wearing pigtails. He checks the windows and doors and locks, runs fingers through his thinning hair, places his hands on his hips, and tells me to call again if I need to before he closes the door.

We start participating in the neighborhood in small ways. We stop by the tree regularly. We shop at the local grocery store. And when a child support defendant insults the mother of his child for where she lives, I look up the address and say, "Oh, that's just two streets over from me."

But it is my father who connects the dots for me about the significance of sharing a neighborhood with the women I'm representing. I don't realize that I am straddling his past and my present. How he longed to live in community with the patients he was treating. And I don't know that I am once again following his footsteps come the end of the summer when I can choose to leave. I don't recognize the privilege of choice in the same way that I'm rarely aware of my skin tone. I still don't see what Gerry would have liked me to see—that choosing to live in a place for a summer is not the same as having urban planning, politics, skin color, income, and history choose for you.

* * *

But there is one night when my eyes open a bit wider. The summer I live in D.C. is the same summer that John Grisham's novel *A Time to Kill* is released as a movie. Pete and I go to watch it at Union Station after grabbing burgers and Cajun fries at the food court. Movies have always been one of my favorite languages. My mom used to take me out of school for important films. In Germany while on my pilgrimage to her family I'd watched *Sarafina!* in Freiburg. Her cousin and I walked out after two hours, blinking like bats in the bright sunshine, my popcorn still half-uneaten, my stomach turning in on itself. I had expected the dancing and harmonies of my childhood. Not the other truth—what apartheid did to a girl my age because she was Black. A twelfth grader like me who had also hated how the government tried to make Afrikaans the official language of our schools and our mouths. But where my class and I had stayed silent in protest and laughed off the insults of our Afrikaans teacher, she and her class spoke out, walked out, marched in protest, and were arrested. I didn't have a category in my brain for a story where the police plugged teenagers into the equivalent of jumper cables and flipped the switch. So I tried very hard not to think about it. Because I could choose to. Because I knew it would never happen to me.

We are almost the only White people in the theater the night we watch *A Time to Kill*. I remember how I felt when I read the book. I remember my revulsion and my rage as a girl and also a wannabe lawyer. But in the theater that night we are surrounded by the rage of a Black community watching the rape and lynching of a Black child by two White men. My own righteous indignation stutters and is utterly eclipsed by a wave of voices interacting with the film. And when the rapists are gunned down by the grief-stricken father, the place erupts. It feels like a cross between a courtroom, a charismatic church service, and a political rally. I feel my whiteness like a neon sign in the dark. It is like my window is rolled all the way down and this is a story I can't opt out of. Because instead of movie characters I see my friends and neighbors, my clients and their moms and dads and grandmas and aunties clapping and crying and pumping their closed fists in the air in the *Amandla!* Power! *Awethu!* Is ours! call-and-response that was born in the South African rage against apartheid. The theater is a swell of lament, and Peter and I are drowned in it.

And in the street outside this theater, in this city that makes me feel deeply at home with its foreign embassies and languages and foods and people who all know the name Nelson Mandela, is also the comfortable reality that when Peter walks home late at night through my complicated neighborhood, followed too closely by street hustlers, the police have been known to pull up and offer him a ride to the metro in their cruiser. Justice is never something I've had to take into my own hands. Instead, it's always held the door for me.

When we walk out after the movie, it's darker and later than we anticipated. Those were the days we never had money for cabs. So we walk faster. A car pulls up next to us. The music is throbbing through its doors, and a young black arm emerges, waves Peter over.

"Hey, y'all know how to get to Anacostia from here?"

Pete ducks his head down to the level of the front passenger window, talking to the four guys in the car, giving turn-by-turn directions in the days before Siri. I hear laughter and then the engine guns and the car peels away from us. We keep walking. The night feels heavier, like it is rushing us, pushing us toward home.

From across the street, we hear someone yell, "Hey! Hey, what'd those kids want?"

There's a man waving wildly and swearing at us. We walk faster. He keeps yelling, "Hey, I'm talking to you! I'm motherf**kin' talkin' to YOU!"

He yells louder and jogs across the empty street toward us, and it's impossible to pretend he isn't there. In a neighborhood well known for its homeless population, its drugs, and the shootings we see on the news where our block regularly shows up behind police tape, we know better than to be out this late.

He's caught up to us now. He's older, he's Black, and he's irate when Peter explains where the guys in the car wanted directions to.

"Are you motherf**kin' stupid? You think they don't know where that is? They comin' back around for you. You gotta get outta here!"

We're nodding, still walking as he keeps pace with us. He's wearing a tan jacket and it flaps around him like a cape as his arms windmill in frustration at our stupidity. "You're walking around here all motherf**kin' white, light, and bright at night. Do you wanna die?! You gotta get inside!"

We stumble on our words and our feet and nod and move faster, and he breaks away from us as we turn the corner left off North Capitol onto M Street. My heart is lurching as we climb the steps up to my building and through the front door and into the living room with its beanbag chair and stolen cable.

* * *

At the end of the summer I move out of the apartment and two of our Black friends from college move in. I'm headed back to Boston for my junior year, and they've just graduated and are staying in D.C. for work. They tell me they've never lived in a Black neighborhood before. I look at them with a blank face and wide eyes. All summer they've laughed at our stories of disorientation, and once over dinner they seemed to relish the night that could have ended badly for us because of our whiteness.

"Now you know how it feels" is what I got when I was expecting sympathy. It stung like a cut you haven't noticed until you go to wash your hands. My reply got stranded in my throat. And anger knocked. But I didn't open the door. I remembered.

I remembered one of those same friends making angel food cake and defrosting frozen strawberries as I sat at her kitchen counter in her student apartment downstairs from mine earlier that spring. The place had smelled like sugar and comfort, and she was bending over to take the cake out of the oven when she told me what our White classmate from Virginia had said.

"We were talking about where our parents are from. And I guess she realized our families come from the same area."

She put the baking sheet down on the counter and reached for the packet of strawberries and started to cut them open as she kept speaking. "So, then she laughs and says to me, 'I bet my grandpa owned your grandpa.'"

She shook her head as she poured the sticky berries all over the delicate sponge cake.

I stood up and said, "No way! She did not!"

"She sure did. Just laughed like it was nothing."

She cut a slice and scooped up a generous slathering of strawberries and handed the bowl to me. I took it, staring at her, shaking my head back and forth like I could shake those sentences out of my mind.

"Yup, she said that ignorant thing and then just kept right on with the conversation."

We ate the cake and the berries and tried to swallow the bitter with the sweet. That was in the spring.

In the fall I still remember how both tasted.

So when anger knocks now, I don't open my door. I roll down my window. I think of Gerry. I try to see.

* * *

My dad arrives in August to visit and drive me up to Boston and back to school. I take him to meet the neighbors under the tree. It's an instant connection. They invite him to the neighborhood keg party. He's never seen a keg before, and his delighted curiosity, British accent, and big personality are instantly embraced. It's like a superpower, his ability to chameleon into a new culture. He's taken into an apartment I've never been invited to and proudly shown the keg. He loves it. He is very tempted to stay, but we have a long drive ahead of us. It's also the first time my two Peters meet. Two opposite forces in my life. One loud, one gentle. One quick to anger, one slow to speak. One commanding, one introspective. Both carrying my suitcases out of the corner apartment with the bars on the window and into my dad's rental car.

We pose on the scorching hot asphalt for a photo with our college friends outside our old apartment and their new apartment, and then my father gets into the car, giving the man who will become his son-in-law a chance to say goodbye and a look that says, *I don't expect to see you ever again.* Peter puts his arms around me, and it will be a year before we live in the same state again. I feel his biceps like an anchor about to be lifted, leaving me adrift and unprotected again. I breathe him in—Polo Sport, soft cotton, cinnamon gum, security—and the tears I'm embarrassed to cry in front of my father make it hard to swallow. He imprints his body against mine. And he kisses the salt from the corners of my eyes and, with his stubble pressed against my cheek, tells me, "Everything's gonna be alright."

CHAPTER 9

What Our Scars Mean

The drive from D.C. to Boston will take us four days. My dad has a medical conference in New York City that will make his time here a tax write-off.

We pull out of the parking lot, and Peter's white T-shirt and dark blue khakis are a Monet painting shimmering in the rear-view mirror. Traffic absorbs us and my father's focus is on navigating the mixing bowl of highways all trying to escape the city. History flashes past my window as we drive away from my future. I feel a great emptiness in the car, the space between my father and me like a language barrier it will take me all four days to cross. I've been speaking the flush syllables of first deep love for six months now, and of independence for the two years before that, so today I lisp and stumble over my words as I try to move back into the tongue of my childhood that I'm not fluent in anymore.

My dad and I are aliens to each other and this country as we travel its longest north to south interstate, I-95, which stretches the length of the East Coast of the United States from Miami, Florida, in the south to Houlton, Maine, in the north. We will cross miles of stories I won't come to know until two decades later when Peter and I are knitted permanently together, bone and flesh and babies, and bring our family to a house in Maryland, planted almost exactly halfway between Baltimore and Washington, D.C.

The I-95 corridor will take Dad and me through my future and his past from Baltimore, Maryland, through Philadelphia, Pennsylvania; New York, New York; Providence, Rhode Island; and finally up to Boston, Massachusetts. I watch the skyline shape-shift from monuments to smokestacks to skyscrapers. The car with its bossy seatbelts that bark at us with a high-pitched yap every time we stop for gas or snacks and forget to leash ourselves back to the seats is a time capsule. We cross the Mason-Dixon Line that decapitated the Northern states from the Southern, and I know nothing about this line in the sand between Maryland and Pennsylvania. I know that the air feels like a giant dog tongue licking me all the way up my spine and on up the back of my neck. My dad is full of conversations I don't want to have and questions I don't want to answer. Charles Mason and Jeremiah Dixon are ghosts outside my window, and my internal borders are shifting as I survey who I was and who I am becoming, as daughters have always done.

It took four years, four centuries ago, for the Penn family of Pennsylvania and the Calvert family of Maryland to settle their long-running boundary dispute that had brought Mason and Dixon from England to act as surveyors. And one hundred years later, farmers, laborers, barbers, mechanics, schoolteachers, fathers, and sons from opposite sides of the line would fight and bury their blood on the fields of Gettysburg, Pennsylvania, in the final and fatal attempt of the Southern states to breach the Mason-Dixon Line during the Civil War.[1]

We are all tourists in someone else's history.

The first time we stop for gas, I wait in the front seat, staring out the windshield. My dad leans back in through his window. "Lisa-Jo, how do I do this?"

I swivel, distracted, in his direction. "Do what?"

"Work the petrol pump," he says. At home filling up with gas is a full-service experience. Attendants in BP uniforms whistle up to the side of the car. "Full up?" they ask. "Check the oil?" they inquire while you wait in the driver's seat, pass over a credit card, scrounge for change for a tip, and pull back out again without ever having handled the pump yourself.

"How do you get the pump to work?" My dad is bemused as he gives the machine a once-over.

"How should I know? I've never had a car here." Irritation, like sweat, is a soft shimmer covering my skin.

My father figures it out. Gets back in. Puts the car into gear, and the seatbelt immediately barks at him. He shifts back into park, pulls at the belt, laughing, "Okay, okay, I'm doing it," and clicks it into place. He's still laughing as he pulls back out onto I-95.

"Man, if they'd asked me for a couple hundred, I'd have handed it over." He's looking over his shoulder as he merges. "That was so weird to fill up a whole tank for so much less than at home."

My smile is uninterested. I don't see what's outside my window. I don't see what's inside my window either; I'm too focused on what's inside my head. My dad has a map on the seat next to him, but it is a mute guide to the places we pass through. It doesn't tell us how much we have in common with this land of unfamiliar gas stations and freeways with their yellow central line instead of the white markings we paint down our highways at home.

Maryland is behind us, and the four lanes of traffic are rushing away from my semester off campus. I stretch my legs out in front of me. My flip-flops have fallen off, and despite the scorching D.C. summer I'm still as pale as I've always been. I cross my left leg over my right. My dad is focused on the flow of traffic. We're passing through shifting terrain; Baltimore's gaping harbor seascape of shipping industry and smokestacks has given way to gently rolling hills of oak forests as we cross the Susquehanna River and on through Amish country toward New York. I shift in my seat. The topography of my left leg below my knee includes a soft, shimmering scar, like a micro-lake, that ripples with skin distinctly different from the shoreline of the rest of me. I trail my index finger across those delicate waters. I close my eyes. I remember.

I was twelve. It was Dorothy's birthday party. I was as familiar with her house as I was with my own. Our parents could have been interchangeable by then, we'd been growing up together for so long. Her house was my house. Her pool was my pool. Her party was my party. I was wearing my eighties pastel pink shirt with the sleeves rolled up paired with a white bubble skirt. My mom dropped me at the end of the driveway rather than embarrass me by driving all the way into the middle of the party. I was late. There were kids everywhere. That was back when my baby heart had loved Grant Forest since third grade when I once helped him thread his needle during a sewing project. Now in sixth grade, I didn't object when someone suggested a game of "kissing-catchers." Instead of "tag, you're it," you got to kiss the person you caught.

I wanted Grant to kiss me. But I was also fast. My chest and my knees pumped with breaths and steps and exhilaration, and he was always just there, just at my shoulder as I ran, checked, reversed, spun, and twisted under the pine trees, their needles and gum sticky under my toes. And my head was spinning, giddy with glee right up until I slipped and tripped on the brick paving around the pool and he pumped the brakes as I skidded and sprawled at his feet. Self-preservation kicked in right as all that red hot blood from my cheeks started spurting out of my shin.

"Whoa, you okay?" Grant's hands were held out in a kind of surrender, a kind of protection in the air above my leg.

"Yes, no, I'm fine. It's okay. Really." And I wasn't quite lying because the adrenaline was still keeping the voice of the screaming pain that was about to crash into my afternoon trapped in a back room.

I could tell he wondered if he was still supposed to kiss me. But he had caught me only because of a forced error, and so instead he hovered and said kind things to crowd out the embarrassment that was crowding around me along with Dorothy and all the other kids from the game. I stood. I smiled. I hobbled inside. I left a trail of blood. The kiss I never got left a deep scar that still shimmers from my skin thirty-eight years later.

My dad had stitched me up. First, he'd given me the *umjovo* to numb the wound, the needle playing hide-and-seek inside the hole in my skin. And slowly, expertly, he'd threaded the suture needle and pulled the damaged skin back together with a row of neat stitches like medical kisses. My father, as it turns out, was the creator of the little lake with its delicate skin that was left behind on my shin. He knows this. The scar that should have been a hair's breadth had spread like a rift valley, the skin eroding, stretching, until it had made a small dam of new DNA where the old, dead, and damaged skin hadn't been properly cut away. He had tried to stitch together skin that was beyond repair. So my body had embraced the disrepair, the stitches stretching farther and farther apart, like hands slipping out of each other's grasp, the skin getting thinner and thinner, until what was left was a soft, delicate shimmer the size of two quarters. What my father sees now reflected back in that scar is his own work that didn't hold.

I look at his profile as we edge toward New York City—this man who molded me out of his DNA, language, geography, and passion. There is nothing halfway about my father. He is the gas pedal all the way down all the time. To be near him is to be in motion. When my driver's license and my mother's grave were both still brand-new, he put me behind the wheel on an annual road trip back to the Karoo, with its highways that stretch from horizon to horizon, and barked at me anytime the speedometer dropped below 180 kilometers per hour (120 miles per hour). I drove with both hands on the wheel, dry sweat in my armpits, my father in the passenger seat commenting on my lack of courage, and my little brothers in the back seat. Foot flat.

On I-95 my dad changes lanes. With authority. He is a force field of conviction.

The deeper story is that I drove that car at eighteen like I was driving NASCAR because my dad believed that I could. He has always been stitching his belief in my abilities into my skin. I am marked by my father's faith in me. A speeding car, a

prestigious internship, admission to a top-twenty law school—
his answer is always the same: "I knew you'd do it." Period.
The end. He believes, and this almost always makes it so.

We stop for ice cream. I slip my feet back into my flip-flops
and open the door. The humidity is still there like a wet, cloy-
ing hug harassing us as we move between the air-conditioned
car and the air-conditioned convenience store.

My dad is walking the aisles with a look of concentration
on his face. "What's that fruit juice you always tell me about?"
He's staring at the giant collection of refrigerated drinks that
stretches the length of an entire wall.

"Nantucket Nectars?"

"Yes, that's it." He leans in and picks Orange Mango and
Kiwi Berry and Guava, all the glass bottles he can hold.

"And what's that ice cream that everybody likes?"

I understand what he's doing. He wants to taste the culture
his daughter has been assimilating. "Ben & Jerry's."

"Yes," and now he's opening the freezer doors to see past
the frosted glass and into the rows and rows of options. He's
surprised by the mini self-serve sizes.

"Isn't this the kind Pete likes? The cookie dough?" He's cra-
dling a container in his hand.

"Yes. That's his favorite. But I don't like it. I think it's weird
how they put cookie dough and peanut butter in everything
here."

My dad's eyes catch the glint of gold wrappers in the
freezer.

"Chocolate Magnum! Yes!" He grabs the king of preten-
tious ice creams and puts our snacks and bottles down on the
counter. He is still handing over more cash than necessary; the
constant currency conversion is its own kind of language that

takes time to learn. He gets his change. Carefully puts the receipt in his wallet for his accountant. The bottles are jangling in the bag from his wrist as we walk across the steaming parking lot and fold ourselves back into the car and obediently buckle up.

He tries the juice first. Takes a big swig. "Good grief." His mouth purses in displeasure. "This isn't juice; this is just sugar water." He's looking over his shoulder now, backing out of the spot. "I mean, where's the fruit? At home the juice has so much fruit in it, you can basically chew a mouthful of Liqui Fruit. This is pathetic."

I immediately feel defensive. "But the different flavors are so fun."

He's merging onto the highway. "It's like fruit-flavored water. No substance." It's a statement. Like everything he believes, there is no alternate opinion. There is only his truth and then what everybody else thinks. I pop my cap. Instinctively I read the note that I love about these bottles, buried like hidden treasure in the lid. My brother Joshua once had the goal of getting a random fact about himself printed in those bottle tops. I drink my juice and my irritation.

My dad is done with the insipid juice and is now scrounging in the plastic bag between his legs for the ice cream. Gripping the steering wheel between his knees, he bites the corner of the gold wrapper to peel it back and reveal the thick, rich chocolate shell enclosing the vanilla insides. His eyes flick back and forth between the road and the decadent ice cream. He bites off a massive mouthful, exhales blissfully around the first bite. He talks out of the corner of his mouth. "Mmf this is good. How's yours?"

I want to enjoy what I'm eating, but my mouth is full of a

surly resentment I can't seem to swallow. I'm sitting in my own personal eclipse as my Northern Hemisphere drops into darkness as the shadow of my father passes overhead. The sweet strawberry shortcake popsicle in my hand is a tug back to the campus where I first tasted it and where my father has never visited before, the place where being his daughter is not my primary identity, the place where we are inexorably headed.

The highway is zipping by, the sky outside the windows shifting to dusk, the brash summer colors muting, and inside the car my father is so sure of himself one minute and then the next is shifting into a softer palette that I haven't seen before.

He grunts and the hand holding the still mostly uneaten Magnum drops down to his thigh. I feel his foot ease off the gas. The car and I are both unsure.

"What?" I ask, looking over at him. I'm still speaking annoyance.

He's holding his mouth in an awkward way, not swallowing, not talking, and I forget to be irritated and become interested. "Dad, what's going on?"

"I bit my tongue." He's trying to drop the half-eaten ice cream into the flimsy gas station plastic bag that is uncooperative, and I reach over to hold open one side so he can get rid of the dripping stick, flicking his eyes between the road and the bag. I pull the bag over to my side as he leans back in the seat, his long legs stretched down to the pedals, his right hand now rooting around in his jeans pocket for the handkerchief he always carries with him. I'm watching and still not comprehending what's happening as he brings the cloth up to his mouth and puts almost the whole square of cotton in.

"Dad? You okay?"

He takes out the hankie and we both see the almost obscene amount of blood soaked into it at the same time. He puts it back, presses down on his tongue.

"Holy cow, Dad. How did that happen?" I find a small ripple of compassion rising to the surface.

My father is still driving, still pressing the hankie down inside his mouth, still focused, but now I notice how his edges have softened and I glimpse the man inside the father.

"I chipped one of my canines a while ago and I keep biting through my tongue because of it. The dentist tried to file it down because the last time the cut was so bad I needed stitches."

I had no idea. I haven't heard this story before. He takes out the soaked handkerchief, glances down, looks back at the road, rotates it, and puts a corner that's still mostly white back in.

"Wait, so do we need to go, like, find an urgent care or something?" I feel the temptation to irritation rise back up in my chest. This could be a long and complicated detour for two foreigners without U.S. medical insurance.

"No." He talks through a mouthful of cotton. "I'll just keep pressure on it." He keeps driving and doesn't complain. It's then that I'm surprised to realize he is in pain, that he has pain he has to manage apart from me. I am uncomfortable trying to comfort him. I'm still tender from the years when comforting him was my full-time job after my mom's sickness sliced through him. I am leaning on my left-hand side in the seat next to him, watching him drive and blot his tongue, and I let my leaning in speak for me.

* * *

It's dark when we arrive in New York City. My father's handkerchief is rust red. His tongue has stopped bleeding. The streets are confusing, and I don't help my father navigate because I can't. I can only sit in the front seat of this car because it is taking all my concentration to hold these two parts of myself together that I feel stretching painfully apart, between my D.C. Peter and my South African Peter. There is a slicing pain through my forehead, and I rest it against the glass of my window as my dad pulls up to our hotel. We're only a few blocks from Central Park and I should be more excited.

We check in and I am disoriented by this merging of worlds: New York City from the movies and my father from the farm in a country on the opposite end of the world. His enthusiasm is also dialed down, his tongue a hindrance to conversation. We drop our bags in our room, and he pulls back the curtains on a city that is the furthest thing from familiar. I don't want to meet it. I want to lie down.

"Are you hungry?"

"No, I feel nauseous. And my head hurts." I'm crawling under the blankets with difficulty; they're tucked as tight as a straitjacket on the bed. "I wish I had some crackers and Sprite and maybe some aspirin."

This is a useless statement because my dad is not one to coddle. Nor to care about pain that doesn't come with a side of stitches. So I am surprised when he doesn't insist I get up and come to dinner with him. But I am too tired to care about being pretend polite tonight. I hear him go into the bathroom and rinse his mouth with water. I hear the toilet flush and then his bag unzipping as he roots around for a light sweater. He does this all in the semidark, the room illuminated only by the million lights from the skyscrapers outside the window.

"I'll go down to the front desk and ask where I can get some

Sprite and crackers and pain meds." He says this softly and then I hear the door click closed. I lie in the dark and wait for time to pass.

After my mom died, I stopped sleeping. It wasn't a phase. It lasted from the last months of high school long into my sophomore year of college. I would put off going to sleep as long as I could because of the dread of the boring, dark hours waiting for me. It was like a kind of claustrophobia—the aloneness and the dark and the boredom. I was afraid of it. In my last months of high school, I would avoid my twin bed that was next door to my brothers with their bunk beds and I'd hover in my parents' room as my dad got ready for bed. His dental hygiene routine was long and painstaking, and I knew it would give me another half hour at least with company. I'd sit in the armchair on the side of the bed my father now slept in alone under the duvet with the poppy flower print my mom had picked out.

I'd hear my dad floss and gargle and rinse and spit and repeat and then he'd be climbing into the double bed, his bedside lamp still on, casting shadows on the ceiling, as I sat tucked in the armchair beside him. He'd sit with a pillow propped behind his head, his long white forearms with their prominent veins folded across his white T-shirt, his heavy eyes turned in my direction.

I'd keep up both sides of the conversation as he slowly slipped lower and lower in the bed, the pillow shifting behind him, and every now and again I'd panic as his lids closed and squeak out, "Dad! You're not asleep, are you?"

And he'd blink and squint and reply, "No, no, I'm still awake, my darling."

I'd keep talking and talking while watching his eyelids, propping them open as long as I could by force of will and syllables.

He took me to see a sleep doctor and a dietician. Because I couldn't seem to figure out how to make food go down either. She sat in a chair across from my father and me and leaned forward and listened as I described how I was fine, really. "I just can't seem to figure out how to swallow. I mean, like, how to get the food to go down because I'm never hungry."

My dad was listening more than he was talking, and this was a strange anomaly. I knew he knew that my sleeping and eating patterns were disjointed and as bony as my hips, so he kept quiet and we both waited for the doctors to cure me.

"You could try shakes," she suggested. "They're high in protein and easy to make." She smiled at me like she'd solved the problem.

"But it's not the food," I tried to explain. "It's kind of like I just can't get anything to go down."

Language is limited when it comes to grief. You can't easily sum up in sentences a total loss of appetite, of the ability to continue being human in a human body with human needs, when your soul has decided it is no longer interested in participating in the exercise of being human.

"Like, I just can't seem to swallow."

My dad was watching me and he looked tired. I was also tired. But I was not sleepy. I didn't know how to fall asleep like I didn't know how to swallow. These basic skills of toddlerhood seemed to have left with my mother.

"Have you tried creating a nightly routine?" the sleep therapist asked.

I raised an eyebrow.

"It's a way to teach your body how to shut down. You start it even when you're not sleepy. And going through the steps every night in the same way helps rewire your brain to know that what comes at the end of the routine is sleep."

I was curious. My dad looked skeptical.

"So you could always take a shower or a bath. Put on the same lotion that has a soothing smell, something like chamomile or lavender. Then brush your hair. Listen to music. Step by step, taking your time, until you finally get into bed. You'll find your brain learns to turn off when you teach it the steps."

It was like learning to walk again. Learning to live with grief and the hole left by the person who left me.

I began a nighttime routine at eighteen that I'm still practicing at fifty. The therapist was right; it would become a series of cues prompting my brain to turn off for the night.

In the future when my husband, Peter, is in the bed beside me, I will learn that his brain doesn't work like that. His is a light switch; he can flip it off in seconds. Mine still powers down over hours. But even today, as I slowly rub the Pond's face cream into my cheeks as I have been doing for decades, I feel sleep tiptoe into the room, along with memories of my father's nights sitting up with me.

I'm still wide awake when the hotel room door clicks open and my dad comes in and turns on a table lamp. He doesn't have crackers or Sprite or aspirin.

"I couldn't find anything that was open. I walked up and down Fifth Avenue, but it's all jewelry and clothing shops. I couldn't find a pharmacy or a grocery store or even a gas station."

But he's got a tall Styrofoam cup, and I see his long fingers performing silhouette pantomimes on the wall as he unwraps a straw and pokes it through the lid.

"I stopped at the hotel bar to ask if they have strawberry daiquiris."

I'm so surprised I sit up. I'd told him about Fat Daddy's in D.C., the spot Peter and I loved, where we drank virgin daiquiris during the semester and sweet rum-filled ones in the summer.

"They didn't have strawberry, but they gave me this. It cost fifteen dollars," he tells me. I take a sip. It's a sickly sweet orange flavor. It doesn't taste familiar. But it tastes like a truce.

"Thanks, Dad. Really."

* * *

New York City to Boston is a five-hour drive. The conference on leukemia has wrapped, along with my father's commitment to attend the ballroom sessions on the disease that killed my mother. We have made the obligatory trip to Central Park. I still feel adrift between two worlds, but as we cross into Massachusetts and leave I-95 for Route 128 north toward Gloucester, familiarity creeps into my bones. We pass through Peabody, Danvers, and Beverly and take exit 48 for Grapevine Road. I guide my dad to Conrad Hall, one of the New England style homes that has been converted into housing for upperclassmen.

It's quiet on campus. People are arriving back after the summer in slow waves, and my dad unloads me and my suitcases.

"Okay, I'm going to go find my hotel." We've eaten dinner on the drive, and it's late and we're both tired. I hug him good night and am relieved to unpack my dirty laundry and my thoughts alone.

He arrives early the next morning. This is the campus and college he's been paying for, and it's his first time to see it. I'm surprised when I see him because his professional jawline is covered in stubble and the sun is squinting through his haystack of hair that looks like it hasn't seen a comb or a mirror yet today. And below the surface of our conversation, I feel a current that pulls me to consider that maybe he slept in his car and not a hotel. I resist it. I don't like how it makes me feel—a strange combination of embarrassment and sympathy. Years later he'll tell me how every single place he called was either booked or comically out of his price range. We never paused to consider the impact of hundreds of parents returning their kids to school on hotel rates. So he'd found an anonymous spot in the way back of the student parking lot, hidden by the low-reaching pine trees, and made an awkward bed in the back seat.

I walk him to the library with me; my first class is at eight. I'm not sure how to get him breakfast and get him situated in time for my class. But just inside the doors are a few of my friends I haven't seen since the end of fall semester and my off-campus spring and summer in D.C.

"Hey, Lisa-Jo! You're back!"

I'm surrounded by a few of the guys who are also studying English or political science, and we hug and I introduce them to my dad. And of course, from the moment he opens his mouth and that accent with its intensity and curiosity comes out, they are enchanted by him. I tell them I'm late for class. They tell me they're going to take my dad back to their dorm.

I'm uncertain but also relieved as I hand my father over to their care.

Three hours later I walk from the library all the way off campus, following the bends and curves of Grapevine Road, to the last campus-owned house where the boys live. I've never been there before. It's shrouded in male mystery, and I haven't ever felt confident enough to step across the threshold. I walk up the drive to the side of the house, open the wooden screen door, and find myself in the kitchen. And there, at the worn wooden table, sits my father, holding court. The guys have made him tea and breakfast, he's clearly showered and shaved and changed, and every seat at the table is taken as he tells stories.

They look up, surprised to see me. With wide eyes, the poli-sci cynic I've known since freshman year laughs and turns to me and says, "Your dad has some unbelievable stories." They all chime in with nods and laughter, passing my dad cookies and asking him to finish the story he's in the middle of. I take a seat and see my father through their eyes. He is gentle but holds himself with the carriage of a king. His hands are sophisticated, and when he cups his mug of tea, you see how well groomed his fingers are. His voice is a dance of inflections, bringing the story to life, and the table hangs on his words. He smells like fresh cologne and sounds like your favorite college professor, the one who is the antidote to every mind-numbing lecture you've ever attended. He is impossible to ignore. And the dust motes caught in the midmorning light dance in front of us like the spell he is weaving over these young men.

I sit and watch, and my heart creaks open with a sudden shove of love for this man who has made me in his image. For better and for worse. I feel a strange sensation pressing against my chest, and as I put my elbows on the table to lean in and listen with the rest of the group, I recognize it as a kind of surprised pride.

The most surprised I have ever been by my father was the one time I humiliated him the most and he didn't lose his temper. I was fifteen, my mom was still alive, and my father was my Sunday school teacher. And in a fit of teenage ridiculousness and a crush on the boy who played guitar for our youth group, I had flicked a gumdrop high into the air in the direction of my crush. I watched that candy arc through the air before it dropped, landing squarely on my father's head, where, to my horror, it stuck in his hair.

The class laughter was immediate and shocking, and the blood in my veins accelerated as I watched my father's confused face. And as I realized he had no idea why we were laughing, I felt shame soak my veins. I reached up quickly to pluck the gummy out of his hair, into my palm so I could show him the joke he'd been missing. I remember how his eyes met mine and then swept over the class and tried to herd the teenagers like hysterical cats back to the lesson. It was a futile exercise. And then the waiting began for the tsunami I knew had to be headed my way.

But on the car ride home, over lunch, and all the rest of the week the often-troubled waters of my relationship with my dad stayed still as glass. So I forgot. Until the next Sunday when, after my brothers had inhaled their roast chicken and mashed potatoes, my parents asked me to stay back, telling me they wanted to talk to me. I shifted in my *riempie* chair and waited. My dad looked at me and said in a completely calm voice, without even the smallest smoldering ember, "I was so hurt by how you treated me last week."

My eyes grew wide and my mouth went dry.

"I've waited all week to talk to you because it was too painful to bring up. But I wanted to let you know how I felt, when I looked around that class all laughing at me and looked at you for help, and all I saw was my own daughter laughing at me too. Lisa-Jo, I was so deeply embarrassed. It was so humiliating."

And across the dining room table, across the Spode dishes with their beautiful pattern, across the leftovers and the crumpled-up napkins, I learned a true thing: I learned that my father was human with a heart that could be hurt, just like mine.

So, as I watch him now across another kitchen table, as I hear the delight in the voices, see the admiration in the eyes, the fascination with the man who was brave enough to let me go halfway across the world to write my own story, I feel pride and love so heavy that my heart and lungs drop into my stomach to make space for them.

I tuck my knees under the table. I run a fingernail through the crumbs littering the surface. I am listening to my dad and I don't fully realize yet what I am learning. But I am learning that some scars are not the opposite of love. Sometimes they are the proof of its passing through. Where love is stitched into even the most painful stories.

CHAPTER 10

The Language of Violence

I graduate college and I go to law school because I am still trying to solve what feels like the unsolvable equation: I want a way to cancel out injustice for justice. So my Peter and I drive the secondhand Ford Tempo that we bought the same day I graduated, and that my father will always refer to as our Ford Temple, from Boston, Massachusetts, to South Bend, Indiana. The air-conditioning stops working somewhere in Ohio. The roads I traveled with my dad, my fatherland, my Peter of origin I partly retrace with my Peter of choice, the man who is becoming my new country, and Indiana waves us in with her oceans of corn and unobstructed skies that help my horizon-starved lungs breathe deeply again. The gravitational pull of the Midwest, with her open plains and big skies, syncs true with my South African plumb line for beauty.

I roll down the window. I have been traveling to law school for a decade now. Since I drove through Soweto with Gerry and then watched him cross-examine a witness in three different languages and we ate Peri Peri Chicken and chips and drank Schweppes Granadilla soda afterward. Or was it before that, when I sat in the living room with my dad and brothers glued to our TV with the rest of the country watching Nelson Mandela walk out the front gate of the Victor Verster Prison twenty-seven years after he began his sentence on Robben Island, our Alcatraz?

Maybe it was before that even when my mom stood in our driveway and told me that the only way to change our country was from the inside out: "We have to change the laws to change the country." It was the day she took our gardener, Piet, to the hospital. After two White men accused him of stealing the bike my mom had bought him for his daily commute. After they'd whipped him with their leather *sjamboks*. After they'd stolen his bike. After I'd said we should go to the police and she'd told me there was no point. That the apartheid laws wouldn't care. That we would have to change the laws first. That change had to begin from inside the system. When people won't surrender their prejudices, the law has to insist by rewriting their available options. We don't travel different paths from our parents unless we take new routes. New laws make that possible.

I lean my head back on the car seat, and the wind has whipped my hair into tangles, my short sundress still too hot for the oppressive day and the baking interior of the Temple. I close my eyes against the sun and let the memories crawl in from the dark caves at the back of my mind. Maybe this trip, this traveling to law school, this longing for justice, began before that even, back when I was eleven and all fifth graders were sent to *Veldskool* (literally translated "bush school" in Afrikaans)—like summer camp, if summer camp took place during the public school term in the winter and was run by ex-military types who were raising up the next generation to be able to recognize land mines, build a shelter, and stand guard against the *swart gevaar,* or "Black danger," they told us was creeping toward the White suburbs.

We were none of us quite ready for a training bra, and yet we spent seven days at a school-sanctioned wilderness camp being taught military discipline and the state religion of apartheid.

I had been carsick when our bus pulled into the campgrounds at dusk. We'd spent three or four hours stranded in a grocery store parking lot en route because our bus had developed a knot in some part of its intestines and we'd had to wait on a mechanic to untwist it. So we had crawled in late and tired and I still had a knot of nausea looping around my own insides. The place was run by men we called the *ooms,* or "uncles," dressed in camouflage fatigues, who began barking at us as soon as our scrawny arms had hauled our suitcases off the bus, the last school out of four or five groups of fifth graders to arrive.

"*Wikkel, wikkel, dames!* Hurry, hurry, ladies! You're late. You missed supper already. Get your gear. Find your friends; get into teams!"

And we shuffled and hustled and dragged our bags as we grabbed on to our friends like life preservers while the sea of hostile accents swept over our confused English voices.

There are two White tribes in South Africa, separated by language—a dividing line deeper than any shared skin color. The Afrikaners, descended primarily from Dutch immigrants fleeing religious persecution in Europe and following what they believed was God's call on their nation to be His new Israel. And the British colonizers who brought their empire, their redcoats, and their scorched-earth battle tactics to subdue the Afrikaners, who were resisting the Commonwealth, insisting on their independence and right to vote, and claiming the country's gold and diamonds as their own. Two brutal Anglo-Boer wars later the British withdrew, but the scars of their concentration camps and tactics against women and children left on the Afrikaner consciousness would never be erased from our accents.

"Okay, good. Look at you, hey? Now, let's be serious," and then the *ooms* started picking us off, one from each group of friends, to shuffle the deck, force us into new packs. I looked around at the group I'd been rounded up into and recognized no one. But I saw my expression reflected back at me in the face of every other girl: confusion, worry, a touch of a stomach twinge.

"Listen up, you have twenty minutes to take your suitcases up to the dorms and fetch your rucksack and get sorted out before we hike to base camp." And the night blurred then and I stepped into a bad B movie, lining up for my military-grade rucksack, trying to tie a sleeping bag on top of the gut I'd stuffed way too full of way too many things I wouldn't need and would regret hauling through the dark by the time we hit the first kilometer out of ten on a trail that was pitch-black beyond the few feet our flashlights could pick out at a time. I carried my sleeping bag most of the way since I hadn't had time to tie it on properly. The long line of tween girls spread out like a column of ants marching through the night, without pause or break for adjustments or the fun that is supposed to accompany camping.

I watched my white sneakers with their pink piping stepping foot after foot through the dirt and the red dust, and my shoulders ached from the pack and my arms had started to resent my sleeping bag and my throat wanted to burst out into laughter when I saw myself in my mind's eye, like some kind of girl-child Frodo or Sam trapped in the relentless march of the orc army through Mordor. It couldn't be real. The joke was on us—daughters of the redcoats who marched across the deeply resented history of the *Veldskool ooms*—and their pleasure at our discomfort seemed to warm them more than the fires they taught us to build at camp.

I don't remember us having tents. We gathered pine needles to make soft nests for our sleeping bags. And took turns standing "guard duty" throughout the night in two-hour shifts by the light of the Southern Cross. It was never clear what we were guarding against; what could eleven-year-old girls do anyway if confronted with danger? The fear that stalked our camp was on the inside, not the outside.

My breath was damp on the four A.M. air when my teammates shook me awake for my shift. I climbed out of my cocoon and slipped into my *tekkies*, my sneakers, and walked to the pine tree where I was to keep watch over the totally silent landscape that watched me right back. Groups of tween girls slept in hollows under the pine trees, and I wondered if the *ooms* would know if I left my post. I let my spine fuse with the tree and imagined myself growing stronger just for it having my back.

They marched us back to the campgrounds the next day, and there was talk of a small tuckshop, or snack station, where you could buy chocolate or chips or soda to supplement the standard-issue camp food. When I stripped the rucksack off my skinny, chapped shoulders, I dove into the suitcase I'd left behind on that first night and came up empty. My wallet, my money, my watch—it was all gone. And the five days that now stretched between me and home became a pill that I couldn't swallow, and reluctantly the frustration and disbelief of the last two days slipped out of my eyes and streamed from my nose.

"Gillies!" The *ooms* were yelling for us in their accents that turned *r*'s into *l*'s, and "girlies" became "gillies." We lined up with our bags and half-empty backpacks and some clutched packets of chips in their hands as we stood in long lines that snaked through the dormitories. And we were counted off and separated, room by room, eight at a time, with military precision.

I shuffled forward with the line until I was at the front of it, and the *oom* directing traffic snapped his head around and reached out with a thumb and forefinger and grabbed my nose between his fingers. "What's this?" he said, pinching my nose and rubbing the wetness between thick fingers. "Is this snot, hey? You crying, my gil? What you crying for?" But he wasn't interested in my answer. And I let my hair swing down across my face as he laughed and pointed to my bunk bed, and I walked away down the hall and laid my bags across my mattress. Every morning and every evening there was room inspection, and while most of us hadn't had our periods yet, we learned to fold military corners on our beds and bizarrely watched enough slide shows on weaponry that we could recognize an AK-47 and could list the most likely places a land mine might be buried in our neighborhoods.

It was like being in Cadmus's surrealist rendering of the deadly sin I was most familiar with out of the seven, *Anger*. The painting is of a giant, bleeding, screaming monster, many of its wounds self-inflicted, its rage bloated and irrational, anger for anger's sake. If I'd been familiar with the piece at the time, I would have said it had come alive in our campgrounds on the afternoon one of the *ooms* stomped up and down the lines of little girls under his care assembled for drill inspection and, when one of them let out a nervous giggle, barked, "You think this is funny, hey? Listen, my gils, listen: if you don't take this serious—I kill you till you dead. You hear me? I kill you till you dead!"

It was almost funny. Almost.

Of course, I didn't believe him. But I struggled to tell that to my loose stomach. By the time our bus came back to take us home, we had marched and guarded and leopard-crawled and learned that there was an animosity that stalked every syllable spoken by the Dutch men to the daughters of their British colonizers.

When our bus pulled into the visitor parking lot at the front of our school, I had my forehead pressed to the window, watching for my father to come into sight. I saw his familiar green station wagon before I saw him in the crowd. I was struck by how civilized he looked in his dress shirt and tie. I didn't know how I would put the week into words for him when I knew he was expecting to hear tall tales of camp hijinks and joy.

I walked through the crowd of parents to the soft pocket of sunshine pooling around my father, and I could smell the sap from the pine trees above him. He was grinning so wide, and I tried to shape the syllables to give words to the week. I was a child who spoke the language of violence and didn't expect to find it so hard to verbally shrug about the experience.

I was surprised to find my body insist that it was only eleven. My words never made it as far as syllables, and instead a deep cry worked its way up my throat. I remember the feel of the brown buttons on my father's sweater as I pressed my face into his stomach and stood and swayed and cried.

He reached down to me, and his eyes hardened to flint. "What happened? Tell me!" And as I continued to cry, he said, "I'll *kill* them." Maybe that's what he said. Maybe that's just what I want to remember he said. Maybe that's what his facial expression was saying. What I knew is that as much as I'd often feared my father, it was nothing compared to what I realized he would direct against anyone who threatened me. I don't know what my dad said to the school. I do know that the location we attended was shut down a year later but only after a kid died. I remember feeling a desperate kind of vindication when the news snaked its way through the school's whispered grapevine—yes, yes, that place was the danger; *Veldskool was the danger.*

* * *

When my father was eleven, the same age I was when I went to *Veldskool,* he learned to fight. My grandpa had strapped twelve-ounce boxing gloves onto my dad's young fists and taught him and Gilbert, the neighbor boy whose dad ran the farm community's petrol depot, to bob and weave. Grandpa crouched down in the old barn, grabbing them each by the scruff of the neck, and said, "Listen here, boys, you have to be able to box if you're going to make it at boarding school." So my dad learned a right hook before he learned long division.

There were 150 boys boarded in Arthur Kingwill House, the school hostel that had been my dad's home away from home since the second grade. Fights exploded like land mines under the feet of teen boys, and my father can still remember the first and last names of every boy he fought.

It was a genteel *Lord of the Flies:* small White boys shipped from their farms in the middle of nowhere to get an education at the boarding school in town with its civilized blazers and ties and tea time every afternoon at three P.M. Boys gathered in the outdoor quad for hot tea that was served in porcelain cups from a giant urn that already had milk and sugar added in generous doses to the mix. Snacks of dried peaches or *biltong,* South Africa's beef jerky, or rusks were foraged from tuck boxes, the treasure chests that held a boy's supplies from home. All ages and grades of boys from second through twelfth were shoving and pushing to get their cup under the single spigot of tea, and my father was in the thick of it. A completely ordinary boarding school afternoon of his eighth-grade year.

Except for Ivor Roux.

Ivor was in twelfth grade. A Goliath his parents had tried to tame by extricating him from gang life in his coastal hometown of Port Elizabeth and shipping him inland to boarding school, where he was also taking tea on this particular day when my young father turned, cup of piping hot tea in hand, and collided with Ivor's immovable middle. The hot, sticky beverage soaked into Ivor's shirt as my father made eye contact with the giant. No words were exchanged. Ivor's hand spoke volumes: He hit my father across the head—an open-handed slap. With the urn to his back, my dad was trapped, and like a mouse in a cage with a cobra, he knew he was in trouble.

He got his teacup down on the table before he was hit again in the head, and as he turned to try to get out of the way, Ivor headbutted him on the nose and my father's eyes exploded in sparks. He staggered backward, trying to get out of the huddle, out to the expanse of the lawn, when Ivor hit him one more time. My dad says he couldn't see properly by then, felt himself trip against the stairs leading down to the grass; he was starting to believe he was going to die, that Ivor could kill him under the bright Karoo sunshine surrounded by all his friends.

He didn't dare hit Ivor back; he just wanted to get out of his way, when he felt a hot hand press between his two scrawny shoulder blades, propelling him forward again, right smack into the wall of Ivor's furiously heaving chest. "Leave Rous alone." The words came from behind my dad. And he recognized the voice of Froggy Young.

Also in twelfth grade, Froggy got his nickname from his obsessive workout rituals and all the weights he lifted that had turned his legs into a muscular landscape that was the stuff of legend at the school. Also from Port Elizabeth, he was a soft-spoken fitness fanatic who had decided on this day to intervene. My dad darted to one side and still Froggy's words hung in the air: "Leave Rous alone."

"Why should I?" Ivor had shifted his focus to Froggy.

"Because I say so," came the reply.

And the predictable counter, "Who's gonna make me?"

And the equally predictable but deeply miraculous, *"I'm gonna make you."*

And suddenly one boy took up the chant: "Barney! Barney! Fight! Fight!" And one hundred pubescent breaking voices all joined in the chorus.

The prefects took charge, organizing the fight. "Okay, boys, off the grass. Everyone off. Get back. Back up to the tar."

The head prefect said, "Froggy and Ivor—you're on the grass. One-minute rounds. Fists only."

And then another addressed my father: "Rous, you can stand behind Froggy."

My father shuffled to Froggy's side of the manicured lawn, and a prefect yelled, "Go!" The sounds of flesh on flesh competed with the shrieks of boys. There was no hesitation; they simply started pounding each other in the face: my father's savior, Froggy, and the local Goliath. A symphony of sounds— the fleshy slapping of a fist landing in a face; the deep, guttural echo of a fist on a chest; the almost silent sound of a fist sinking into a stomach.

After the first round, my dad ran to bring Froggy water. Small, ineffectual hands trying to be helpful, fanning the body of the bigger boy with its bright red welts. Froggy didn't even look at my dad.

"Rous, bugger off, man! Bugger off!" he grunted.

My dad was so desperate to make sure Froggy didn't lose. He stood to one side while a couple of Froggy's classmates wiped the snot and blood off his face, the sweat out of his eyes.

The second round was terrible.

In the third round Froggy hit Ivor hard enough to knock him down. And my dad exalted. He leapt off the ground. He screamed. He punched the sky. He went wild. Ivor staggered up. Froggy knocked him down again.

"Stop, okay, boys, stop. That's enough." The prefects stepped in and stopped the fight. And my father always says, "But my life was saved." He tried to approach Froggy. To say the words, "Thank you, Froggy. Thank you, man."

But Froggy had just two words for him: "Bugger off!"

After that day whenever the tea bell rang, my dad would watch for Froggy, circling back every teatime to offer fealty to his hero. He was usually camped out at a table, surrounded by his friends, and as they sipped and swore and played with the windup engines they'd built, my dad would go back time and again to his tuck box for treasures for Froggy. He'd take out a rusk or piece of *biltong* or dried apricots and watch from a distance, waiting for a gap in the conversation, and quietly approach Froggy, standing close enough to slip him the small offering of a saved soul, no words exchanged. Froggy would just palm it, and my dad would keep walking.

At the end of that year, after graduation, all the Port Elizabeth boys were loaded onto a flatbed truck to be driven to the train station. The school was buzzing; all the kids knew the truck was coming to take a large crop of their upperclassmen for good. My dad's eyes were trained on the truck. Boys and bags and suitcases were being loaded onto the flatbed, and the engine was slowly turning over, preparing to pull out of the school's driveway. Froggy was one of the last to board. He had two huge suitcases and was hauling them to the back of the truck just as his shadow, my father, followed behind. And as Froggy turned, my father's hand was there, fiercely determined to pick up those bags and load them, though they strained all his muscles.

Froggy watched, never saying a word, as my dad staggered under the weight of the suitcases, shouldering them up, up, up, and over the lip of the tailgate, one by one into the hands of the boys already aboard, who hauled them the rest of the way into the bed, where they were safely stowed.

Froggy never took his eyes off my father. And spoke just two words to him: "Bye, Rous."

"Bye, Froggy. And thank you."

Froggy swung himself into the truck bed, settling down between the other boys. And my father said he kept his eyes on Froggy until they couldn't see each other anymore.

* * *

Justice is a shape-shifter. That's what I'm learning. In my first year of law school we study in circular question patterns, our professors always poking holes in our reasoning. I find it confusing. I want the blueprints for justice. I want right and wrong to stand still in a lineup so I can identify them. Instead, like my dad, I learn to shadowbox—in my case with ideas, with arguments. While the letter of the law might mean one thing, the spirit of the law, I learn, could have a completely different definition. Some days it feels like a shell game: the competing case law a kind of legal sleight of hand. It seems there is no black and white. There are only shades of gray, facts never rock-solid but always open to interpretation.

I would have been tempted to be discouraged if I didn't also learn that there will always be people trying to solve that unsolvable equation. People who won't quit working the problem till they can cancel out injustice. There might always be bullies, bigots, strangers demanding you be on your guard against nothing more than their own fear. But there will also always be children wanting to know why. There might always be relatives still serving up their inherited rage with the roast beef and mashed potatoes. But there will also be moments of clarity when we refuse to keep consuming the same narratives as our parents. There might always be Ivors, but there will also always be Froggys.

In my criminal law class we study the case law around torture. I don't like it. I can barely read it. I go to my professor to ask him for advice. I knock on his door. I explain that I don't know how to read, let alone memorize, this world of deliberate, intimate, embodied violence. I want to know how a soul isn't suffocated by inhaling this kind of smog, even just for research purposes. Like an inquisitive kestrel in a nest of legal tomes, his chair swivels in my direction, along with his eyes. His eyes that have seen so much more than mine. I haven't worked for a big litigation firm yet. I haven't defended a corrupt governor yet. I haven't billed my time in obscenely expensive six-minute increments yet. I haven't lived in Ukraine yet. I haven't worked for the United Nations yet. I haven't met women who left that country to be dancers or waitresses or nannies and instead ended up in hole-in-the-wall apartments looking down the barrel of months of sweaty, pounding, thrusting johns and pimps and flesh dealers yet. I haven't studied truth commissions yet. I haven't sat in on the hearings of the South African Truth and Reconciliation Commission (TRC) yet. But I will. I still will. And justice will become harder to wrap my head and my hands around. I haven't begun to look my native land in the eye yet—not my father and not my country. But I will. I still will.

At nearly fifty, when there are wrinkles around my eyes and my lungs are caked in layers of the soot I couldn't stomach in law school, when I've read the obituary of my criminal law professor, and when I start writing this book, I will look fully into the eyes of my father and see our history clearly. It's not easy—for either of us. My black-and-white categories don't work anymore—the *them* I tried to put on the injustice side of the equation bleeds into the *us* I have always put on the justice side. I see that when it comes to justice, there is no *us* and *them*. When it comes to evil, there is no *us* and *them*. When it comes to violence, there is no *us* and *them*. There is no way to opt out of the parts of our history that put us on the wrong side of the equation. As much as we might want to. There is no *us* and *them* because there is only one beating heart of humanity— a single organism connected by vital arteries of history and memory and one divine and holy breath breathed into all of us. We are an interconnected species. What my father's people did for good and evil decades ago lives and breathes in me today. And what my people did in South Africa lives and breathes in the family trees of America. I live on both sides of the equation.

I learn this slowly, over years. And then I stumble onto a crash course the afternoon my dad unlocks a door in his story for me that I've never entered before. I walk inside a room I didn't know existed and feel the shock of what I find like a punch. The story he tells me took place on an otherwise ordinary Sunday afternoon seven decades ago. He was about to be served roast mutton and potatoes on his uncle's farm, north of Middelburg. The extended family was gathered for lunch. Mutton. Crisp potatoes roasted in fat. Carrots glistening with butter. My six-year-old father. His parents. His cousins. They were all gathered on his mom's brother's farm: my great-uncle Gerard's farm. Oom Gerard. I had never met him, never visited that farm.

But my father takes me there in his story. I watch it unfold and become part of my story. The Xhosa maids have laid the table with the Spode and heavy silverware and silver napkin holders and the stiffly ironed cloth napkins I am familiar with from our own farm. Food is being carried in from the kitchen with its own Aga stove. The table and a small boy's stomach are both groaning when a maid bends down and whispers in Oom Gerard's ear as he holds the carving knife and fork poised over the leg of lamb, *"Baas, hulle soek jou buite. Onthou en Klein-boy is terrug.* Boss, they are looking for you outside. Onthou and Kleinboy are back." Oom Gerard drops the carving implements and pushes his *riempie* chair back from the table, its legs dragging, his napkin falling to the floor.

"Finally!"

Earlier in the day, before lunch, before my dad had even hugged his aunt and uncle hello, Oom Gerard had gotten word that two of his horses along with their bridles and saddles had been stolen by farmhands who'd taken off in the direction of Middelburg. He'd been checking in with the police, and before lunch the phone call had come through on the party line to report that the men had been caught.

"Ons stuur hulle terrug na jou," the local police officer had said as Oom Gerard stood in the hallway, receiver handle grasped tight. "We're sending them back to you." After catching them, harassing them, threatening them, the police had barred their way to Middelburg and herded the two men back to the farm.

The table is buzzing. My tiny father vibrates with the room, translates the mood, understands that there will be consequences.

Oom Gerard heads for the door. "I've got to go sort this out." He addresses his brother-in-law, the women, and the children, "I'll be back just now. Wait for me." Everyone nods, agrees. The meal is put on hold as Oom Gerard stomps outside, doors slamming behind him, my father's curiosity anxious to follow. He is still inside but can hear the shouting in the courtyard, the barking of a hysterical dog. And this is the moment. This is the beginning. This is when my father is baptized into the vocabulary of violence. He tells me, "I knew then."

His voice is soft. I hear the six-year-old speaking through him: "I knew that there was a terrible monster outside."

He had been told to stay inside, threatened on pain of death. But a terrified curiosity pulls him like a riptide, slowly, surely, out the back door, around the corner of the house, and toward the single-car garage with its wide-open door and cement floor. He's wearing khaki shorts, and his *veldskoen* leather shoes are soft and nimble on his quiet feet as he edges closer to the garage, as if summoned by the monster. The sun is bright and the sky clear, the scene painted in everyday colors. The open garage. Oil stains on the cement floor. All the tools of farming hang on the corkboard walls. And in the middle of all that ordinary are the two farmhands and Oom Gerard holding a *sjambok*. That uniquely South African whip made from adult hippopotamus hide, the leather shaped to be wide at the handle, narrowing to a fierce tip. Oom Gerard's massive Boerboel dog, similar in build and fight to Grandpa's baboon dog, Robert, is quivering at his side. And then there are Oom Gerard's sons and finally the two Xhosa men who'd taken the horses, Onthou and Kleinboy. There is one other Black man my father doesn't recognize who is doing something my father can't make sense of.

My small father, his Sunday shirt sticking to his back, hides in the shadows, watching the room, the cramped space, its very walls straining to hold the confusion and jostling of men and dog and sweat and fear and fury and the presence of the terrible invisible-visible monster. Slowly, deliberately, the anonymous man is lashing the left arms of Onthou and Kleinboy together. They try to resist; Kleinboy is pleading, *"Ag jammer, Baas, jammer. Aw, sorry, Boss, sorry. Ons het nie die perde gesteel nie, net geleen. We didn't steal the horses, just borrowed them."*

Onthou is talking frantically with his hands held up in surrender: *"Luister, asseblief, luister.* Listen, please, listen." But the dog is crowding them, and Oom Gerard is making them submit under threat of his whip, and slowly their flailing arms are being turned into a single unit of human flesh. My father watches from the corner of the house with wide baby eyes, unable to look away, and hears his uncle say slowly, deliberately, savoring the words like the tender, rare lamb they had been about to bite into for lunch: *"Nou gaan julle mekaar bliksem."* There are some things that feel impossible to translate. Our family trees are one of them. These words hang in mine: "Now you are going to fight each other."

Onthou and Kleinboy are strapped together and staring with confusion at Oom Gerard.

"En as julle nie veg nie, gaan ek julle blerrie bliksem en ek sit die hond op jou, jou donnerse diewe. And if you don't fight, *I'm* going to bloody beat you and set the dog on you, you damn thieves." And the monster grins, a sloppy, lusty face as the two men start to try to hit each other with their free arms, bound together like a three-legged race, designed to kick and trip itself.

They are unenthusiastic at first. Circling each other, landing a slap or punch with their free hands. Until Oom Gerard whistles for his dog and sets it on them.

"Veg! Fight! I said, fight, dammit!" And his whip cracks through the polite Sunday afternoon and splits Kleinboy's skin through his tired work shirt. And the two men panic and start to attack each other in earnest. There is the sound of flesh on flesh. Fists. Grunts. Curses in Afrikaans and English and incoherent isiXhosa words swallowed up by the desperation to survive. My father watches from the shelter of the house as the

two friends are forced to fight each other. But the monster leans in close to my father, breathes in his face.

Oom Gerard watches; his face is flushed, and sweat beads along his upper lip, and he's impatient and aggrieved and lit up from the inside as he screams at them, *"Veg, jou bliksems!* Fight, you bastards!"* And then he loses his patience and lets fly his own arm and works his *sjambok* across their backs, their arms, their thighs, and his dog lunges, canines sinking into scrambling legs. The men scream and rotate in a tight circle of punches and gasps and feet shuffling on the cement floor, blood mixing with the oil stains, the dog yapping and salivating, their backs blossoming with bright red branches and leaves on fire. Oom Gerard is sweating and swearing and working his whip. It is an orgy of violence.

Then Kleinboy, the name that means "small boy" in Afrikaans, like a South African Little John because he is huge compared to his name, roars. The whites of his eyes roll back in his head in panic as he leverages their shared third arm to lift up his friend Onthou and slam him into the cement floor with the thud of soft flesh on hard concrete. Kleinboy is heaving and keening and ripe with the smell of sweat coming off his body. The sweet smell of fresh blood is a cloud that drifts toward my father, who has stopped breathing as he watches, hypnotized by his family.

Onthou doesn't get up. Kleinboy is still attached to him, pulled over by their shared arm, bent at the waist, heaving and gasping, still tied to the friend he has smashed like a pumpkin. Onthou—"Remember" in Afrikaans. The monster grins at my father, and that's when my father runs. He runs away, his body shaking and bile pushing up inside his empty stomach. He runs back into the warmth of the house, where the women and the meal wait. But the lamb will have to wait longer. The pickup truck roars to life as Onthou is loaded up and dropped off at his hut, like a sack of grain. Then Oom Gerard returns to the farmhouse and the lunch that is still waiting for him. And my father hears him wash his hands down the hallway before he joins everyone back at the table and takes up the carving knife again. Everyone sits down to the four-course meal, served by the maids, eaten with perfect table manners, and followed by coffee and chocolates and Sunday afternoon naps.

It is later, when the White family is well fed and well rested, that the maids come to bring news that Onthou hasn't woken up yet. That there is water leaking out of his ear. And the six-year-old boy who grew up to be my father and fought his way to a medical degree can now recognize the spinal fluid that was leaking out of Onthou's ear. He now understands it must have been from a fracture at the base of the skull that happened when his friend was driven to smash him into the floor.

Oom Gerard isn't gone long. He drops the unconscious Onthou off at the municipal hospital. Tells them that "he fell." And that "he bumped his head." I have no idea if he waited for Onthou to be admitted or how he explained the other injuries. Just that he shared these few facts with the curious family when he came stomping back into the living room, where everyone was taking their evening sherry. "Bloody nuisance," he says as he takes a deep sip of his liquor.

He'd loaded Onthou onto the back of his pickup truck like Grandpa once loaded his baboon-mauled dog. But no one held Onthou's head in their lap. No one tried to stop the bleeding or the slow drip of spinal fluid. No one was in a rush; no one from our family seemed to care if he came home or not.

But unlike Robert, Onthou would never come back to the farm. He would develop meningitis and die slowly at the hospital. And my dad would never tell his uncle or his cousins or his father what he saw. And if there was a funeral for Onthou, I don't know. I don't know if Onthou had a wife or children. My grown-up father simply tells me in a voice that carries the weight of memory, "I've never told anyone that story."

When we hang up, I stand at the kitchen counter and feel the nausea roil through my stomach. It churns deep inside me, where I now know I inherited a monster.

CHAPTER 11

Tourists

My name often confuses folk, who think I must be from the Deep South with that double-barrel, hyphenated first name, Lisa-Jo. I like to laugh and say, "Much farther south than that." I say it for years before I learn that, like my name, I share an origin story with the American South. And that despite all my good intentions, despite my name that's as ordinary as apple pie or the girl next door, despite believing the best about which side of the justice equation I am on, despite all that, my family tree still grew out of the soil of injustice. And the branch that bears my name comes attached to roots and a trunk that metabolized and passed on to me a monster. I can pretend that it isn't real, that it isn't mine, that I'm not responsible for its behavior. Or I can do what I learned on the game farms of my family—I can stalk it, I can track its *spoor* through my life, and I can hunt it down. What I cannot do is ignore it. The most dangerous lion is the one you can't see. Because while we cannot kill what we refuse to see, it can still just as easily kill us.

The year before I arrive at law school, Peter comes with me

to South Africa. He steps into the origin story I am still learning. And we sit in a school gym in a small town in what feels like the middle of nowhere and listen to people tell stories that they've never told anyone before. It's one day out of the seven years of post-apartheid Truth and Reconciliation Commission hearings. In the messy deconstruction of apartheid, truth has become more valuable than gold. Truth about how husbands were disappeared, where sons' and daughters' bodies are buried, when mothers could stop waiting for their babies to come home. Truth becomes its own kind of justice. Archbishop Desmond Tutu is fervent in his belief that trading courtroom justice for truth is how we solve South Africa's apartheid equation.

"We had a horrendous past," he famously said. "We needed to look the beast in the eye, so that the past would not hold us hostage any more."[1] So for seven years hearings are held across the country, and instead of an adversarial court system where truth can become a shell game, the Truth and Reconciliation Commission can offer amnesty for violence in exchange for the truth if (1) the act was perpetrated between 1960 and 1994, (2) the act was politically motivated, and (3) the unvarnished whole truth is told. A lie will disqualify you from an amnesty petition.

So every night the news broadcasts the stories into our living rooms, and along with mouthfuls of *pap en wors* or *babootie* or lamb chops, the nation swallows impossible stories of police brutality, political hysteria, and violence that slipped out of pajamas and into police uniforms in the middle of the night and disappeared Black fathers and sons, mothers and daughters, before driving home to serve their White kids Weet-Bix for breakfast.

In the summer between my first and second years of law school I will research truth commissions for a professor writing a book on how torture robs us of our humanity because it robs us of rational words. She will argue that truth commissions give victims back their voices.[2] And on a winter morning in South Africa, I sit in a high school auditorium and bear witness to that fact. The hall is chilly. It doubles as a school gym and a theater with a stage at the far end of the big, open room. There are rows of folding chairs separated by an aisle down the middle. It's like a wedding with guests divided on either side: families of the victims on the left, families of the perpetrators on the right.

Small booths are set up all along the left-hand wall of the building. They look like phone booths, but they contain the translators who will interpret the testimonies so the assembly can listen to the stories in their native tongue. Peter and I are given headsets when we come in. They look like the kind of Walkman tape player we used as kids. There is a channel you can change to find the language you need. I can understand all the English and Afrikaans, but I need translation for any of the other national languages. We've driven nearly three hours from the capital of Pretoria to the city of Pietersburg in a car borrowed from my father. A trip to my homeland is what Peter asked for as his graduation present. I had told him I couldn't marry him until he knew me, knew where I came from. I barely knew myself. But I knew enough to know that traveling to bear witness to one of the TRC hearings in person was vital.

The hearing begins like a church service. A candle is lit. A prayer is breathed over the gathering. A single chair is set center stage. A microphone placed in front of it. A table with three commissioners sits stage right. And one by one former members of the Security Branch of the South African Police— those secret police notorious for their broad powers to track down, detain, and torture suspected opponents of apartheid without trial—will file up to the stage and take their turn sitting in the witness chair and telling their story. They are wearing three-piece suits and wide ties, and I watch their ordinary faces and think of Steve Biko, who was beaten to death in Security Branch custody; he had been detained at a roadblock.

The officers are confident. Their testimony borders on bored. I think it irks them to be made to give an account of their activities. They tell the auditorium that they were executing a standard roadblock when they opened fire and pumped eighty-five rounds from their Casspir armored vehicle into a minivan of six young men, members of the military wing of Mandela's outlawed African National Congress, who were crossing illegally from Botswana into South Africa.[3]

The Black families in the front left row cry on and off throughout while the White families on the right sit ramrod straight, wives next to their husbands, hearing maybe for the first time where their men went when they crawled out of bed in the middle of the night or on the mornings when they should have been home, celebrating their wives' birthdays.

The sun moves across the school as one by one the same story is told by different officers. They insist that they followed protocol, that they protected their country from terrorists. As the light hardens to a cutting late-afternoon glare pouring in through the high windows, the commission takes a recess. The posse of former policemen stand up, go outside, and gather in a small circle of cigarettes and smoke on the dead yellow grass where children usually play tag. As the sun slips lower, slowly more facts slip out, and each testimony extends the truth to incorporate more and more that had been left out early in the day when the bluster and resistance were more confident.

My ears are chafing from the headphones and still we sit and listen, and our ears absorb the words coming out of the mouths of men who look like my father, my grandfather, my great-uncle, all filled with righteous indignation. Decades later I find the transcripts from that hearing online; with time and technology they've been digitized. I recognize the facts we heard in person as I scroll through day one. Then I read the rest of the case, the four days of testimony that followed after we'd traveled back home. And I track the *spoor* of truth that had seemed so faint on that first day. And I understand what I saw.

Surrounded by the artwork of schoolchildren and honor roll panels on the walls, stories that had been hidden for decades crawled into the light. Truth may set you free, but it can cut and punch and leave you bleeding and weeping and wishing you could unhear its voice. Truth is a father who testified to the years of police harassment—of spying and threats and warrantless searches—that his family endured during the years his son was living in exile until the day the young man and his five friends who hadn't seen their families in years were lured back into South Africa by the police and straight into an ambush. "For them to be killed like that, like vermin, absolute vermin, was a terrible thing."[4] He called the place "slaughter corner."[5]

Truth is a mother, bent double, her *doek* (head wrap) leaning low over her lap as she took painful breath after painful breath. What we saw on day one makes sense when I read the transcript of her testimony from day four. She asked to keep the evidence photos of her son's body "because when I look at that photo, that is my child."[6] She hadn't seen him since he was chased into exile at seventeen until she saw the photos of his twenty-seven-year-old corpse and finally got answers to what had happened to him. That kind of truth will cut the lungs of a mother with each word she breathes out.

I wonder if the walls of a building can ever recover from absorbing words like that. What happens to a place that bears witness to sentences no parent should have to say out loud? A mother asking for answers to questions she'd been carrying for eleven years. And in a school, a sanctuary for learning, she finally found answers. Like children, we White families were educated by the Truth and Reconciliation Commission hearings. Our ignorance was deafening. I was a foreigner in my own country, relearning my own history.

The commission would refuse amnesty to nine of the Security Branch policemen for failing to "make a full disclosure of all relevant facts"—it was found that they were not motivated by self-defense, as they had claimed, but by a desire "to simply annihilate the deceased upon sight."[7]

We are all tourists in someone else's history, and sometimes it's our own.

* * *

When I graduate law school and get married and adopt America as my homeland, Peter and I move to the Eastern Seaboard of Maryland and make our home just outside Washington, D.C. We will live here for five full years and I will cross the Mason-Dixon Line between Maryland and Pennsylvania time and again on my way to visit my oldest friend without ever giving the history of the place, the name, the people any thought at all beyond the thrill of delight at the visit ahead that rolls in my belly when my car crosses the bridge between our two states. I blare my music in time to my speedometer and enjoy seeing the sign marking the line with the enjoyment of any tourist who thinks they recognize more than they really do.

It's not till a Saturday morning in the early spring, when allergies are plaguing the bronchial passages of many, while the beauty of the cherry blossoms takes the breath away of others, that I feel the first prick of local knowledge goose-bump my skin. I'm driving three friends to a writers' retreat in Lancaster County. The road lovingly cradles the curves of the countryside that is lush as she drops her layers of winter to let us see her vibrant beauty. Talk turns to the two states that this old friendship straddles. And into the warm, languid morning, cold syllables cut through my naïveté: "I feel sick every time we pass this way."

"Wait, what?" My head flicks to the passenger seat, question marks in my eyes. My friend, her strawberry hair long and soft around her shoulders, the cracked window playing with the ends, continues, "Yes, eastern Maryland has strong ties to the Klan." Her voice is slow, methodical. "It felt like it haunted our town when we lived there."

I'm stunned. Dread blooms in my gut. *What is she talking about?* The car concurs: "Maryland has a long history of slavery."

I drive, hands wrapped tightly around the steering wheel, my shoulders warmed by the sun, my mind scrabbling to make sense of this new information.

Later, when we've eaten and talked and shared and unpacked new friendships and packed back into the car and I've navigated my way back across the Mason-Dixon to my tiny patch of Maryland, I open my computer and read and read and read. I am a mother of three, I worry about our bank balance, my contact lenses constantly irritate my eyes, and I love to find a coupon code when shopping online. I am ordinary. I like to think I care about my neighbors. I have tried to solve the equation of injustice. And today I discover that my life still straddles horror stories.

If I am willing to open my eyes, to roll down my window and see them. I am tempted to put my foot on the gas and keep driving. My ordinary Thursdays are already exhausting enough without picking at the scabs of my history, my family's history, my adopted country's history. But here I stand, in my ratty jeans and my husband's oldest sweatshirt, and I can't unsee; I straddle two histories. I make eye contact with them both and I can't look away. Like a mouse mesmerized by a cobra, I am utterly focused on the truth right before me. There is no unknowing now that I know. To ignore what is right before me is to choose ignorance; to pretend the cobra isn't real is to choose death. I want to choose life. So I choose knowing. I choose truth.

On some summer days Maryland is as hot and humid as Ghana. And I let myself feel it, remember it, put the puzzle pieces together in the middle of my White suburban afternoon. I stand on my front doorstep between Baltimore and Washington, D.C., and let the weather take my mind back to the West Coast of Africa, where I once stood inside Elmina Castle on the very edge of Ghana. I didn't go to the castle as a pilgrim. I had never heard of the place. I was there on a work trip, and our hosts had organized the stop at the giant white-washed fort that was once a central slave depot in the transatlantic African slave trade. I was wildly unprepared for the experience.

We'd spent the morning in the treetops, crisscrossing the rope bridges of the Kakum Canopy Walk that span what felt like miles of the forest ceiling, a tourist attraction that paralyzed me with fear. All I wanted was to be back at the hotel, enjoying a cup of hot tea and an afternoon nap. Instead, the minivan pulled into a bay, a cape on the western bulge of Ghana, and the beach stretched out rocky and pockmarked with small wooden fishing boats and gulls and in the distance a castle I'd never heard of. Tens of thousands of people make the pilgrimage to this place every year, but I slid open the van door and stepped out in my sneakers and ignorance and car sickness and felt only irritation that our return to the hotel would be delayed by one more touristy activity, when I was past done with playing tourist.

Kids were selling souvenirs along the path leading up to the castle, but the place felt set apart from tourism. Bleak. Unfriendly. Like something out of a Grimm Brothers tale. The wind swept in from the sea and pulled and pushed us as we made our way into the massive fort. The building is the color of sun-bleached bones. Once known as St. George's, it was built in 1482 as a Portuguese trading settlement and was taken over by the Dutch 150 years later. Gold used to be its currency until human beings became what was mined from the three thousand miles of land between present-day Angola, just one country north of South Africa, up along the West Coast, past the bulge of Africa, to Senegal in the Northwest. The castle fort is a 91,000-square-foot monster that rises from the choppy edge of the land and the Atlantic; it is the "Door of No Return" that millions of Africans passed through on their way to plantations in the United States, Latin America, and the Caribbean. In Arabic Elmina means "harbor." In Portuguese it means "the mine."[8] It meant nothing to me as I entered its shadow, but like my father before me, I felt something terrible crouched and waiting for me there.

I hated visiting that castle. I hated what the guide told us in his slow, measured, implacable voice. I hated the sense of desolation. I hated the small Christian chapel built into its walls, where we stood and learned the history of the place that bought, sold, branded, and traded humans, the rich pine beams under our feet so familiar to the ones from our farm. They were stacked side by side, worn from centuries of feet, with slight gaps in the slats where the sound of hymns would squeeze down to the women's dungeons below, windowless, airless, stifling with the smell of buckets filled with human waste and the strains of worship that were followed by the footsteps of the fort's governor, who would choose a young body to service him after the service.

The only other place I've ever stood where it felt like the earth's own soul had been stained with evil was Auschwitz. Every rock, every beam, every brick, every root, every bolt, every stair, and every roof in Elmina Castle stank of evil. The claustrophobic human holding pens we visited were heavy with a stale air and an impossible weight of grief. The guide herded our small group inside and moved to lock the gates, taller than a man and thicker than his arm. I couldn't do it. I stayed on the outside of the bolt.

Then our guide led us down deeper beneath the stone building, inside the guts of the beast where the basement gave way to a cave. The breaking waves of the Atlantic Ocean rolled in and out of that terrible mouth that had gobbled up tens of thousands of souls into the waiting ships.

"This is the Cave of Tears," our guide shared in a voice that held generations of pain. We stood in a small cluster of jeans and sneakers and baseball caps, all with our mouths tight shut, all watching with wide eyes and ears as the waves groaned in and out of the cold room that had the same feeling of finality as a morgue.

"In this cave, mothers and fathers were separated from their children. Wives dragged out of the arms of their men. Parents knew they were looking their last on the faces of their teenagers, and many drowned on their way to the boats, in their tears or their desperation to escape or to hold on to someone they loved."

The Ghanian guide made eye contact with each of us. My eyes were too ashamed to hold his in that claustrophobic cave. The claustrophobia of the wet stone walls and the low ceilings and the damp, caked layers of earth and evil under our feet. The claustrophobia of the truth that seemed to be pressing back against us as solid as the cave floor, validating the words and weight of a history that couldn't be scrolled past like an uncomfortable Facebook post or removed from a textbook. Because it was the literal reality, a truth as real as the rock we were standing upon.

"Look around. Imagine it. Feel it. How would it feel to hear the screams and cries of your brothers and sisters herded and branded and now separated like cattle, like sheep being sent to the market?" Except I knew no farmer would ever treat their livestock like that—that was reserved only for the people thought of as less valuable than their animals.

It was impossible to feel neutral about that place. I hated it. Viscerally. Absolutely. As a woman. As a lawyer. As a South African. As a Dutch descendant and an American immigrant. As a human being. I mourned that I was related to that place. I wanted out.

Our guide was deeply unconcerned with what his tourists wanted. He wanted the story to shock us, like the sting of a jellyfish tendril that wraps itself around you, embedding until it is flesh of your flesh and bone of your bone and you can't pretend it away by being nice or polite or telling yourself it's not your fault, because you're too absorbed by the shocking pain to be anywhere except in it.

I stood in the cave on the coastline where people my age, with their own claustrophobia and terror and nausea and dread and toddler babies they loved, were forced onto ships, amid indiscriminate chaos, as lovers, children, parents were separated, and many would never live to see the eastern shore of America that I now call home.

*   *   *

I got a violent stomach bug that last night in Ghana. I lay for ten seasick hours listening to the ocean groan outside my hotel room and sweated and retched all my insides out; I lost everything in my digestive tract for so long and so violently that by early morning I didn't have the strength to get out of bed and make it to the bathroom anymore. I simply lay in my soaked sheets, gave up all shame, and let the vomit have its way, my head lolling over the edge of the mattress, the trash can catching what it could. I lay wide awake, my mind still trapped in Elmina, under the castle, in the cave with its terror and tears. I lay and listened to the cry of the waves and the women's voices who would have begged for hope where there was none.

Morning came for me and brought my new colleague, Daria.

"Hello," she said, knocking at the door and coming inside. "I heard you were sick. We're leaving in an hour. We have to be on the bus soon."

I could only lie on my bed and watch her with listless eyes. We had known each other just about a month. We were both South African, me by way of Holland and England and her by way of Persia.

She was tender as a mother with me. "Oh, oh," she clucked as she looked at my pasty face, bloodshot eyes, the state of my bed, my body. She was in the bathroom now, brisk, efficient. I heard the taps running. I closed my eyes. I knew what that room looked like; I knew what I smelled like. I heard her picking up towels, wiping surfaces, putting out the soaps.

She came back to me. "Okay, you can do it. Sit up. Slowly."

She had her arms around me, under my shoulders. I leaned on her warm, strong fullness like a frail grandmother, my body curled up in cramps and dehydration. I was shaking.

"Lift your arms up." She gently eased me out of my soaked clothes and tenderly helped me shuffle to the bath. I balanced on her as I tried to slip into the tub. Slowly, one leg over the edge at a time, I lay down in the water. I soaked in the warmth and breathed in and out and watched my breasts and my hands float on the surface. I heard Daria moving around my room. She was packing. I was naked and utterly defenseless against her kindness. My eyes stared at the tiny window where the sun was a determined new day. I wanted to go home. I wanted to leave Ghana. But as I lay in my dirty water and ex-haustion and naked ignorance, I knew Ghana would never completely leave me.

I stood up and dried off and dressed, and Daria and I walked slowly, painfully slowly, toward our bus, where I would puke for the entire two-and-a-half-hour ride along blood-red dirt road tracks, my body feeling every pothole, every turn, every sweltering color of the sun, as I vomited into garbage bag after garbage bag.

It was almost as if Elmina and its story had crawled up in-side my digestive tract and my soul tried to reject the truth of that place because how do we bear it that our stories are linked? We can be tempted to look away, to put experiences and places and history like that into a tourist's snow globe, reducing their impact, shelving them in the way back of our minds. But instead, the memory of Elmina became inter-twined with my memory of such visceral sickness that it was impossible to distance myself from it. I would still feel that night in my body when I woke up in Maryland a decade later and traced the route from that sunbaked fortress in Ghana to the America I now called home.

It started with the signpost for the Mason-Dixon Line and the day I finally paid attention to the history it was pointing to. And it was followed by the day my youngest had a middle school field trip to the Chesapeake Bay. We'd been through it twice before; both my sons have taken the same trip. They have planned the snacks and comfortable clothes for the boat ride. They have taken delighted videos of the spray and come home to tell me what a fresh oyster tastes like. And for those first two trips, I knew nothing more about the Chesapeake than the facts the boys recited in preparation for their science test about the famous estuary. But by the time my youngest boards a boat for her turn across the bay, I have been reading more than the signpost for the Mason-Dixon Line. I have dug deeper into the history of my adopted state and have finally connected the dots between Elmina Castle and the Chesapeake.

And what I have found is that what began in Elmina ended here in the early 1700s, when tens of thousands of Brown and Black men, women, and children from the West Coast of Africa who survived the crossing were brought by boat to tidewater ports all along the Chesapeake. The Chesapeake watershed stretches from Cooperstown, New York, to Norfolk, Virginia, and includes parts of six states—Delaware, Maryland, New York, Pennsylvania, Virginia, and West Virginia—and the entire District of Columbia. My children have adopted Maryland as their own; they play its sports of lacrosse and soccer and tell me that, once upon a time, jousting was the state's official sport. When the leaves change color here, the entire skyline catches fire, and no matter how many years I drive the corridor of color that is Forest Avenue through our neighborhood, I am never not moved to try to open my eyes wider, gulp down more of the staggering, shocking beauty of this shoreline.

But today I roll my window down and see more of the story of this place. I see slavers who also made Maryland their home, using its waterways to transport the human beings that had been kidnapped from their country, culture, and language. Thousands who had called Ghana home would be doomed to be sold from the Chesapeake to the booming cotton plantations of the Deep South as part of the Second Middle Passage, sometimes referred to as slavery's Trail of Tears. From the

Cave of Tears to the Trail of Tears. It is impossible to be a tourist here anymore.

*   *   *

My father and I both came to America to deconstruct South Africa's state religion: apartheid. But of course, it had long lived on these shores going by other names, climbing out of slavers' boats and slinking into neighborhoods, and sitting down to supper or Bible study or political office or church or book club or PTA in kind and polite places that, while they might not say it out loud, still keep their eyes peeled for the *swart gevaar*, the Black danger.

This is the lie of my childhood—that barriers were erected and Bantustan borders drawn to "keep White kids safe" from the roaring "danger of Blackness." When instead, the violent barriers and the redrawn boundaries were the political equivalent of piracy, as land and resources and the rights of citizenship were stolen under cover of the lie that separate was better for everyone.

It can be too easy to listen to our fears, to our peers, to our parents. To let them drown out the voices rising in lament from behind a wall we don't want to acknowledge is real. Fear dresses up in socially acceptable intentions. And on the morning of April 27, 1994, the year I made the trip to America the first time by myself, it speaks in the voice of my father. It's a historic date. There used to be an entire section in the Newseum, the museum of news, in Washington, D.C., dedicated to that date—the official end to forty-six years of the apartheid regime and three and a half centuries of institutionalized racial segregation preceding that, and the institution of the first national referendum in which South Africans of all races had the right to vote. What he says to me on that date is the perfect contradiction of wanting change while still being afraid of it: "So listen, Mandela's ANC will win. That's a given. We'll want a strong opposition party to balance things out."

I listen to him in growing surprise. I had been imagining my check mark next to Nelson Mandela's face for weeks. I'd assumed we would want to be part of the story of his victory. I am twenty, and it's the first election I am old enough to vote in. I and 19.5 million other South Africans will cast our first-ever votes in South Africa's first democratic election that year. Me because of my age. Everyone else because of the color of their skin. There is an 86.9 percent voter turnout.[9] In the Black townships, people wait in snaking lines that stretch for literal kilometers, and every hour is another step closer to making history. The atmosphere is electric with expectation; this is our New Year's Day, and the final hours of the darkest night are ticking down. The countdown is a spell humming over the full four days of voting; songs fill the air and the smell of cooking fires season the sky as vendors feed the waiting. The day before the voting polls open, our new flag is raised for the first time. On the opening day of the general election our new constitution and Bill of Rights take effect. And the system of Bantustan homelands for the Black population is abolished twenty-four years after it began.[10]

I was born in the Zulu homeland and was almost the same age as that system of land redistribution and separation when it was ended. It's the only reality I have known. But of course, what happens on paper won't change the land lines and the reality for Black families for decades still. There is no backspace key for the disenfranchised—the land stolen, the lives relocated, the families cracked down the middle.

But I get to vote. I get to make my mark on the ground-breaking ballot that has the name of each of the nineteen political parties, along with full-color illustrations of their logo and their leader's face. Apartheid is the reason that entire generations can't read or write, and our ballot bears witness to its long legacy. As does what my father says to me before I head into my high school, which is serving as a designated voting location, to join history in the making. He is preparing me for the day, this man who is South Africa incarnate to me.

"You should vote DP—the Democratic Party. They won't win, but it's good to make sure they have a strong presence in Parliament."

My heart sinks at his words. I feel sad. I am twenty but I don't feel emancipated yet.

I drive myself to the voting station in my father's car with my father's words in my head, and I feel him standing next to me in the voting booth as my hand slides down, down, past Mandela's face, and my pen makes the mark my father left on me next to the face of Zac de Beer—the syllables of his name spelling out the sounds of my Dutch family tree.

And what I don't know yet is that that mark will mark me for the next three decades. Anytime someone asks me about Nelson Mandela or what it was like to live through one of the most radical elections of recent history, I will feel my insides burn with a cocktail of regret and shame and sadness. I won't admit to not voting for Mandela, but I will also never be able to say out loud that I was part of the change. I will always know that I wasn't a freedom fighter in even the most ordinary of ways.

CHAPTER 12

Interpreting

Language is slippery. What we say and what we say and what we mean and what we do can be three paths that all diverge in a wood. To be South African is to be aware of language, since we are constantly moving between at least two, sometimes as many as twelve—treasure hunting for the word that just so exactly captures the meaning you are trying to convey. Translation is a river we are all swimming in, carried by the currents of meaning, both literal and metaphorical. Peter's constant complaint when we are home in South Africa catching up around the supper table is, "Could everyone please just pick one language and stick to it!" He often misses out on the punch line of a joke or the point of the story when the storyteller switches into another language just as they reach the climax, picking the words that make their point with the biggest linguistic punch.

My father loves me. He hates bullies. He has always said how much he loves the Zulu nation, that he despises racism. I believe him. Maybe, though, what he has also meant is that he loves the idea of being the hero. That doing the right thing is most appealing when it makes us look good and feel good.

Paying attention to your words and what they mean and then what you do is a kind of open-heart surgery on yourself. There is a terrible risk: defensiveness and death or healing and life.

In isiXhosa the word *ndiyazidla* means "I am proud of myself." But its literal meaning is "I eat myself." My father and I have been proud of our journeys toward justice, while our unexamined history, our untranslated stories, were eating away at us, like dental decay you don't realize is rotting your gums, your jaw, your insides. And impacting your behavior.

For the last years of her life my mother worked as a translator, moving constantly between English and Afrikaans—government documents or university assignments that needed to be interpreted into the syllables and sounds of English. She would take on extra projects and be up for hours, hunched over her computer in the back bedroom, ranting at anyone who dared to drink the last of her Coke, eat the last of her Cadbury's chocolate. She was fueled by sugar and caffeine and the obsessive need to find just the right word to convey the meaning of the document, no matter how boring or bureaucratic.

I am following in her footsteps, her keystrokes, learning as she did that there is a difference between translation and interpretation. Interpretation requires a careful ear, listening for context, culture, and personal nuance in the voice of the speaker. It is more art than science. As opposed to the more technical act of translation, where one word is matched with a linguistic equivalent in a different language. Translation listens to the words. Interpretation listens to the person as much as it listens to the words.

I have been listening to my father's life since he first delivered me into this world. I have been afraid of him and afraid of becoming like him. And as I stand now on my front doorstep on the East Coast of America just hours away from where he came to interpret our country's story, I am afraid of misinterpreting him. The trajectory of my father's life from the moments when he tried to resuscitate his father's flock of sheep that lay aspirating on the good medicine he gave them in the wrong way has been to doctor. In his hands that word is a verb—*to doctor*. Afrikaans offers a better fit—*geneesheer,* which translated means "doctor." But with only the slightest shift of emphasis on the syllables, the word richens and deepens into *geneser,* which means "healer"—*to heal.*

When medical students intern with him, he always asks them the same question: "What do you think makes someone a great doctor?"

They offer a smorgasbord of answers—technical skill, high grades, ten thousand practice hours, a high-capacity work ethic, self-confidence, and the list goes on and on. No one comes near the answer he is waiting to share.

"No," he always says. "Anyone can check those off a list. To be a truly great doctor, you have to love people." This is what he means when he says he is a doctor.

Love is its own language that has to be learned. Most of us struggle to pronounce its words; some can barely speak in complete sentences. And like all languages, it is easier to learn when we are surrounded by native speakers. We are all lisping our way into love. My father is not an exception to that rule.

There was a tree on our farm along the dirt road between

the highway and the house that had a trunk that looked like it tried to make a U-turn. Where it once grew straight it had taken a sharp right turn before continuing to grow up toward the sky. The tree looked like that because one of my dad's older brothers had crashed into it on a night he was drunk and lost control of his car at that bend in the road, and now there is a permanent bend in that tree. Family trees are like that. We grow up out of the soil of the stories that are so long ago and once upon a time that they might feel unconnected to our regular Tuesday afternoons. But the branches in our family trees keep long records, ring upon ring, of where we come from and who we come from, and they map the ways in which we have changed directions.

We used to make fun of that tree. My father named it after his brother. We laughed when we passed it, a ridiculous land-mark on our farm that made the brother ridiculous. Years of laughter passed unchecked until a day when my father pushed pause on the story. Then rewind.

Then he recorded a new narrative. "That's sad what we did, what I did—making fun of my brother like that. It's ugly. I wish I'd never started calling that his tree."

I listened in surprise. His words braided together what he thought and what he meant and what he did. "That was so ugly, to make fun of a terrible moment in his life."

And it was as if my father shed a skin, like the snakes he used to catch and raise and trade. There it was: the old, dry, shriveled skin of petty meanness that didn't fit him anymore.

I once read how Nadine Gordimer, Nobel laureate for lit-erature, White South African Afrikaner, started asking ques-tions at age nine about the maid who lived in a tiny room behind their house, about the Black men who came to the *stoor*—the small shop in town—and had to pick out their produce and products from behind a wire partition. They couldn't try on the clothes like she could. At fifteen she wrote her first short story, unpacking what she was seeing, typing up her questions in plain sight in her fiction and through her characters.

We are all decoding the characters in our lives, and some of us are brave enough to see how our choices impact the lives of the people we share stories with. The very bravest write new stories. They pick apart their plotlines and find endings that aren't dictated by their bloodlines. No matter how deep into the narrative they are, the bravest believe on ordinary Tuesdays that it's still not too late to write a new ending.

South Africa rewrote its national anthem. Today it is braided out of five different languages that used to be at war—isiXhosa (first stanza, first two lines), isiZulu (first stanza, last two lines), Sesotho (second stanza), Afrikaans (third stanza), and English (final stanza). These are the most commonly spoken of our twelve national languages. Our people have always been divided along language lines, not just by skin color. We have killed the speakers of aspirated consonants. We have rejected kings from across the sea and across our rivers because of their native tongues. And our names spell out our allegiances—to our mother tongue and the color of our skins. But when we are at our best, we aspire to a new history.

Shaka Zulu may be one of the most famous names from our continent, but it is rarely interpreted correctly. The overly romanticized metaphor of his name may have set sail and ended up in the mouths of African diaspora like the student I met in a pub in London who introduced himself as Shaka, that name sounding foreign in his British accent. And as we stood nursing drinks in a loud hallway, I asked him if he knew what Shaka meant.

"Sure—power, strength," he told me.

And I heard my father's voice unfold in my mind, telling me the ancient story of the Zulu Napoleon, who would unite his people into a mighty nation, slaughtering their enemies with brutal military genius. My bedtime stories were woven out of Shaka's feats, his language, and his origin story—how his mother, Nandi, was a Zulu Bathsheba bathing in a river when the king of the Zulus, King Senzangakhona, saw her and took her. She would send word to Senzangakhona months later, telling him that she was pregnant. And the king sent the message back that it was probably just an *ishaka*—a stomach bug. And when her son was of age, she sent him to Senzangakhona's *kraal*—his village—with the message, "Here is your *ishaka*."

Shaka might be a metaphor for power, but it literally means a type of beetle and figuratively means a stomach bug, and it's the story of a bastard child who was first rejected and then terrorized by his father's people until he grew old enough and strong enough to launch his own reign of terror.

Origin stories with their oral histories and layers of meaning are hard to interpret. We might have told ourselves one kind of story for years, avoiding digging deeper and decoding the meaning because we feared it would change our understanding of the story and, worse yet, of ourselves.

For years my father lived in a box in my mind labeled "fear." On nights when my mind was spiraling with the constant ache of homesickness and the itch to be back living in the purple shade of the jacaranda, I would be drawn back to that box, to our origin story. And I would slowly open the lid, and with the smell of veld fires in the winter and jasmine in the spring, memories I couldn't trust would come scrabbling out, like rats in the darkness. I could feel rage, anger, injustice at the story of my childhood running up the inside of my shirt, horrifying me as I slapped at them and tried to stuff them back into the box where they belonged with my father.

With an ocean between us, we could finally live at peace, my father and me. For decades there was a truce thanks to the white flag of distance. Gentler memories surfaced, and new memories were constructed out of long-distance phone calls, building a bridge between us. There were graduations and Christmases, weddings and vacations that brought me back across the ocean and into his home, where we still often rode the seesaw of love and fear, the equation from my childhood I'd never been able to solve. Instead, I focused on taking lots of photos and stockpiling the tastes of *melktert* and Appletiser, malva pudding and *pap en wors*. And my heart would turn nauseous at the airport every time I had to figure out how to say goodbye all over again.

But we never talked about our monster. We never talked about what haunted my memories of being his daughter. To ask him was to risk open war, or, worse, disdain and denial of a truth that had shaped me. So I never told him how angry I was because I didn't pay close enough attention to how much pain was stitched into me alongside his stitches of love, because I never wondered where the anger that seemed to leak out of my pores came from. I avoided interpreting my story. Because I was living my story. I was in the thick fog of sleepless nights with small children and student loans and commuting into D.C. every day for a job I didn't like through the second-worst rush hour traffic in the nation. Years passed in the blur of ordinary life and exhaustion. And like my father before me I defaulted to parenting in anger because that was what I knew. That was my native tongue. Until the day my mini-me stared at me out of eyes sinking below the surface of my rage, and I had a choice: I could push him under the water or I could reach out my hand to rescue him.

And I knew that if I wanted to rescue him, I would have to find a way to rescue myself.

But I was incapable of rescuing myself. History and my own story had proven this over and over. Instead, I recognized that the same God who had raised me up out of the waters of baptism would need to be the one to rescue me from being drowned by the monster that lived in me so that I could rescue my son.

And I took all my faith and doubt, my family story and my desperation, to the God who once inspired the words of another farmhand who worked with sheep and who wrote,

> I waited patiently for the LORD;
> he turned to me and heard my cry.
> He lifted me out of the slimy pit,
> out of the mud and mire;
> he set my feet on a rock
> and gave me a firm place to stand. (Psalm 40:1–2, NIV)

I started to study my son with a mirror instead of a magnifying glass, and I saw him reflected in our shared history—all the passion of his mother and his *oupa*. And I wanted to write a new ending to that story. I wanted our wild, big feelings to be used for good. I wanted the Gospel in me to grow legs that walked out the faith that we claimed and studied and wrote and talked in our family. I was surprised that it could take so long for what we say we believe and what we mean by that and what we choose to do with it to all sync up.

* * *

My dad spoke the language of faith for decades before his actions slowly started to sync up with the meaning of his words. He lisped his way into faith at twenty when he was drafted into the South African Defense Force. He had spent the first month of basic training at Valhalla Air Force base just outside Pretoria, the city I would grow up in. But when he was sent to intelligence operations in the cape, he would meet Fritz Uys, a massive, Bible-wielding Afrikaner. Barrack bunks in Fritz's vicinity were avoided, since no one wanted to be conscripted into a Bible bedtime story.

When my father traces the threads of his faith backward, they end at the Bible in Fritz's giant hands. It was an evening like a thousand others in South Africa's history of eating its Black and Brown citizens in the name of freedom and Jesus.

But Fritz.

My dad had been shuffled up with a change in sleeping assignments and was moved into the bunk next to Fritz. As he lay irritated and desperate for sleep, the deep Afrikaans voice in the bed next to him read the words that make us all family:

"God het die wêreld so liefgehad dat Hy sy enigste Seun gegee het, sodat dié wat in Hom glo, nie verlore sal gaan nie maar die ewige lewe sal hê" (Johannes 3:16, AFR83).

"For God so loved the world that he gave his one and only Son, that whoever believes in him shall not perish but have eternal life" (John 3:16, NIV).

"*Wat dink jy, Pieter?* What do you think, Peter?"

And my father says he'd grown up with a Bible, an appendage as familiar as his own hand or foot, and, like both, it had traveled with him the entire length of the Orange River in his canoe. But having it, reading it, and believing it enough to be changed by it, that part of the limb wasn't operational yet. Dad lay in his bunk, hair still damp from his shower, and tried to get Fritz to pipe down. But so far, none of the new recruits had been able to dampen the big man's enthusiasm for a life that seemed to be free of the military they'd been forced to serve in, the history they were writing, the plotlines that skin and language and a damped-down faith were trying to dictate.

"*Luister, Pieter.* Listen, Peter," and Fritz sat up on the edge of his bunk, head bent over the book in his hands, neck baked a dark rust from the sun, as he flipped to the final story, full of its own wars and dragons and the God who came from a seed of faith inside a woman. And he read to my father:

"*Kyk, Ek staan by die deur en Ek klop. As iemand my stem hoor en die deur oopmaak, sal Ek ingaan na hom toe en saam met hom maaltyd hou, en hy met My*" (Openbaring 3:20, AFR53).

"Here I am! I stand at the door and knock. If anyone hears my voice and opens the door, I will come in and eat with that person, and they with me" (Revelation 3:20, NIV).

And for my father, who would live a lifetime of metabolizing the meaning and doing of those words, this was the beginning. This was when my father was baptized into the vocabulary of faith.

He tells me, "I knew then." His voice is soft. I hear the twenty-year-old speaking through him. "I knew that there was a tender God waiting for me outside my heart."

He was equal parts transfixed by this realization and terrified that someone else would notice what was happening. His voice whispered to Fritz from the dark, asking the question that can change everything—us, our family trees, our countries.

"*Wat moet ek doen?* What must I *do?*"

And Fritz boomed back, "*Pieter, jy moet bid.* Peter, you must pray."

"*Daars agtien ander ouens wat kyk vir ons. Hulle weet jy lees—ek kannie bid nie.* There's eighteen other guys watching us. They know you're reading—I can't pray," my dad hissed back.

"*Okay, gaan buite.* Okay, go outside."

My dad slipped out of his bunk, pulled on a pair of pants, avoided eye contact with Fritz, and spit from the corner of his mouth, "I'll go first. Wait before you come out. I'll meet you under the trees."

My dad tells me that he could feel the embarrassment crawling up his spine, shoving itself into his mouth, swimming down into his stomach. That he felt like a complete idiot. But love has always been the longitude and latitude of fools who are willing to risk what others think of them for salvation.

He was standing under the Southern Cross and the dark branches crisscrossing the sky above him when Fritz followed, uncool and unbothered by pretense, almost tripping on his heels.

"Now what?" my dad said, flustered and frustrated and still unable to walk away from what seemed to be knocking on his soul.

"*Jy moet bid.* You must pray."

"*Net sommer so?* Just like that?"

"*Ya.* Yes."

"No, you pray. It's fine if you pray."

"*Nee, Pieter. Dis jou lewe op die lyn. Nie myne. Jy moet bid.* No, Peter. It's your life on the line, not mine. You must pray."

My father's heart was a racing windmill, spinning wildly in the storm of his changing winds. "I don't know what to say."

"Well," Fritz replied, "just say anything you think to say."

My dad was clueless. His mouth was the Sahara. So he said the first words he could think of. Simple words.

When he tells me the story, he calls them "the most stupid words I could possibly imagine saying." I don't know if he said them in Afrikaans or English. But he said them to the Creator, who is fluent in all our languages: "Oh, God, if You can take me as Your son, please make me one of Your children."

Fritz's shadow blocked out half the sky, and his voice was a one-angel choir: "*Dankie, Here!* Thank You, Lord!" he boomed in a hymn of approval.

My father looked at the man who had invited him into the light and asked, "What do we do now?"

And Fritz's teeth beamed his grin in the darkness. "Well, a new life has started in you, and now you gonna pray every day, read your Bible, tell other people about Jesus."

* * *

Three decades later, my father calls me and tells me a story about Jesus that is like a thick permanent marker relabeling the box in my mind. He is calling about my littlest brother, my adopted brother, added to our family with three other adopted siblings long after I'm out of the house. They will rewrite the story of what a childhood in my father's house looks like. I will not be there to see most of it. But I will catch glimpses. And even glimpses of grace can rewrite whole sections of a life.

The isiZulu word for "grace" is *umusa*. It is also a synonym for "humanity." Grace and humanity. I become related to these unexpected words through my adopted brother and three sisters. The rainbow nation isn't just a term coined by politicians; for our family, it is a phrase that moves into my father's house and leaves footprints through all our stories, even across the box in the back room of the mind of the eldest daughter living an ocean away.

And somehow my father's simple prayer is still causing ripples decades later. He is telling me a story about his youngest son, and it translates into a story about Jesus. "Every night when I get home from work, Karabo asks me if I have brought him a present." My dad's strong British–South African accent is coming through the phone line. I am listening to him, surprised all over again that adoption became part of his story. I have watched it unfold from across oceans and time zones. I have learned that adoption isn't a plot twist in a book. Adoption is a deep story that might one day be told by my siblings. The parts that are mine to share are where God has made us all children of the same family and where our father's parenting overlaps our childhoods.

"So, every day I have to think of something to bring home for him." I hear him shift in his seat, adjust his phone receiver. "At first it was fun, you know? But then it started to feel like a chore and, man, honestly, it irritates me so much." I hear him sigh. I feel my stomach muscles start to clench. I find myself becoming nervous for my littlest brother.

"You know, you want him to be excited to see you! Not just be grabbing at your pockets to find a present!" I hear my dad's voice slip into an aggrieved self-righteousness.

"I was tempted to tell him, 'That's enough. No more presents.'"

I swallow. I feel sad for my baby brother.

But then my dad surprises me, and the relabeling of my box begins.

"But then I had an idea. I found this really cool wooden box. Kind of like a pencil case. With all these designs on it. And I knew how much he'd like it. But instead of putting pencils in it, I found a little mirror and I superglued it to the inside bottom of the box."

My father loves glues. He has a wide collection of all kinds of epoxies and superglues and can fix your shoe's broken sole or that handle that broke off your favorite mug.

"So I finished his pencil case box and I wrapped it and brought it home. And it made me so excited. I was ready for him when he rushed out. He was already asking me for the present before I was even out of the car. Yelling, 'Papa, Papa, you're home! Where's my present?'"

I'm smiling into the room where no one can see me, listening to my surprising father. His voice is also smiling.

"I pushed open the car door and grabbed him and hugged him and said, 'Here, my boy! Here's your surprise. Hold out your hands.' And I slipped the little package into his cupped hands as his eyes were squeezed tight closed."

I can picture the two of them in the garage, my dad down on one knee, Karabo perched on his leg with its perfectly pressed suit pant, together at the top of the steep driveway, the jacaranda tree bearing witness.

"And he opened his eyes and ripped into the present, yelling, 'What is it, Papa? What is it?'"

My dad pauses. I hear him draw breath as a deep emotion runs through his inhale and exhale all the way down to the alveoli in his lungs. I don't say anything. I wait for what comes next.

"He was excited when he saw the pretty box. And I knew his fingers were already trying to figure out how to open it. So I said to him, 'Now, listen, my big boy; before you open it, I have to tell you something.'"

I can imagine Karabo cocking his head, his chocolate eyes locking with my dad's hazel ones. My dad goes on, "I told him, 'There's something very special inside this box. Like treasure. This is a box that doesn't just have an ordinary present in it. This box has treasure in it.'"

And the father I have feared as much as I have loved tells me how my Tswana brother opened the box slowly and found it empty except for a reflection of himself. My heart is now clawing its way into my throat, which is tight with memories and *umusa* as my dad says, "He stared into the mirror and at first he was confused. He watched his own reflection. And then I told him, 'My son, *you're* the present. *You're* the surprise. *You're* the treasure.'"

I swallow. My throat is hot and thick. But I am not swallowing down regret. I am not swallowing down fear. Instead, I find I am filled with almost unbearable joy. It makes even breathing hard.

My father misinterprets my silence. He says my name. My mother's name. My ordinary, terrible, southern, South African name: "Lisa-Jo. My love. I'm so, so sorry."

He's the one crying and I'm surprised, confused.

"I'm so, so sorry I can't go back and give you the dad I am becoming now."

And then my father, my solo parent, is asking my forgiveness. And my ears are echoing with the sound of his voice and my past rotating on its axis, the sound of roaring slipping under the waves of the deep sea of weeping.

* * *

To forgive is not to forget. South Africa bears witness to this truth. To forgive is to see and to know the truth. And in knowing that you have been wronged, to choose to release the rage and the debt of pain owed you. Forgiveness is not an erasing of pain. It is looking the pain in the eyes and honoring it and then releasing it. And it does not require the participation of the perpetrator. But granting forgiveness helps us rediscover the humanity of the person who has wronged us. Asking for forgiveness helps us rediscover our own humanity. This is grace—the giving or receiving of what is not deserved. *Umusa.* Bishop Tutu taught our nation this. And then later I learned it as a daughter.

The grace of forgiveness helps us hold on to our shared humanity. It recognizes and creates room for change. But even if the other person neither sees nor acknowledges nor changes, if we are willing to forgive, we can change our own story. Not overnight. Not easily. But daily, small steps become a long journey in the direction of forgiveness. A long walk to freedom, following in the footsteps of our beloved Mandela, and further back, the footsteps he was following of the Jewish carpenter from Nazareth.

My father is asking my forgiveness. It will be the first of many occasions when his new marriage and his new generation of parenting brings him back to me to bear witness to what was missing when I was the same age as my siblings are now. They will have their own stories of parenting failures, just as I have mine now with my kids. But they will have a parent who speaks love more fluently than mine did, easily offering joy, peace, patience, kindness, goodness, faithfulness, gentleness, and maybe, most significantly, self-control.

When I am homesick for South Africa, I realize I am homesick for my father. For how he wakes up as early as the hadeda bird and for as long as I can remember starts his day with a bowl of muesli, chopping small mountains of apple and banana and grapes to pile on before he pours the skim milk he prefers over it all. I can hear the sound of him chomping through that meal like a satisfied horse. He will smile at me through a mouthful and stand to greet me, and his lean frame is weathered and tough like beef jerky. He always has a tight, sinewy hug for me, and my face will press into the soft leather jacket he wears over the stiffly ironed shirt front that smells of his sharp cologne. He will offer to make me tea or avocado toast, which he's been making for decades before it became trendy. If it's summer, he will sit down again at the table and reach behind him for the fruit drawer, pulling out a peach. But he knows I hate the feel of peaches, so without asking, he'll have picked up a knife and he will painstakingly peel off the fuzzy skin that gives me the heebie-jeebies, slice by slow slice, finally offering me the juicy package that tastes like being known.

Behind me, covering one entire wall of the kitchen, is the new family tree. Planted and watered and tended by the wife and mother who feels like she has always been ours—Wanda is a big part of the reason my father keeps going out on unexpected limbs. And she has printed out their decades' worth of photos of all the kids and grandkids that have blown like dandelion seeds from this house and into the world. Gone are the frames and tiny Letraset numbers connecting the grim and posed sepia photos of my Dutch and British ancestors who cut their way across this country, replaced instead by bright everyday snapshots of the faces of a new South Africa that gather around this table and are family through birth, through remarriage, through grace, through adoption, and through forgiveness.

My brother Luke, my mom's baby born seven years after me, has become my forgiveness mentor. He didn't run away from home like I did. He stayed and paid a price in memories I don't have to carry. So when I talk to him about forgiving our father, I know he knows the cost. I am standing in his kitchen. We are whispering because his daughter is napping. He's pulling on his coat as we get ready to head out his back door, through the garage to his car and out for lunch together. We have been decoding our story together. I'm still blowing my nose and wiping my eyes as I tell him, almost off the cuff, "Yes, I mean, I look at who Dad is now, and I can forgive him."

And then Luke surpasses me and becomes my big brother in faith as he says from his great height, eyes tenderly boring into my own, "Lisa-Jo, it's more than that. Yes, you're right, who Dad is now is great. But I don't just love and forgive him because of who he is now. I also see who he was, and I love and forgive him for who he was then too."

And my throat is burning as I look back over the landscape of my life, and I look back up at Luke. His eyes are full of so much pain and so much love that it's hard to hold his gaze. I know that he's arrived at a country I want to call my own. He's found a place where he can fold together the past and the present in a way that makes my father more human, not less. Luke has shed a skin I'm still wearing.

It's never too late to crawl out of skins we've been wearing that are split and don't fit anymore. Every time my father chooses to listen and bear witness to the pain, past or present, of one of his children, old skins are shed. You cannot stitch together dead skin; it must be shed or cut completely away. Every time I choose to listen and bear witness to the whole of my father's story, old skins are shed, old boxes opened, broken down, and thrown out.

I left to study the injustice against nations maybe because the equation I was always trying to solve was in my own home.

CHAPTER 13

Umusa

Umusa weNkosi uJesu Kristu, nothando lukaNkulunkulu,
nokuhlangana kukaMoya oNgcwele makube nani nonke.
2 kwabaseKorinte 13:14 (ZUL59)

*May the **grace** of the Lord Jesus Christ, and the love of God,*
and the fellowship of the Holy Spirit be with you all.
2 Corinthians 13:14 (NIV)

*Die **genade** van die Here Jesus Christus en die liefde van God en die*
gemeenskap van die Heilige Gees sal by julle almal wees.
2 Korintiërs 13:13 (AFR83)

The African acacia tree, that icon with its umbrella-like branches perfectly silhouetted against a dying sun, makes for great cinematography and also an unexpected link to our family tree. The acacia has adapted in unique ways to protect itself. The tree has developed a symbiotic relationship with the stinging ants that live in its inch-long white thorns. They hollow out the thorns for nesting sites, feeding on the tree's nectar. And in return, if a large herbivore like a kudu or a buffalo tries to take a bite of the tree's leaves, the stinging ants surge out of its branches to protect the tree from being eaten. Maybe this is the instinct of all family trees. To protect ourselves, we make bargains with our rage and pain, our self-righteousness and our righteous indignation, releasing them anytime we feel threatened. We are the self-protectors of our family stories, even the ones with the sharpest thorns.

Perhaps the moment when I began to forgive my father for how he parented me was the day he stopped trying to self-protect. The day he laid down his defenses was the day I could draw near. And it wasn't just one day. It was a series of days over years, in fits and starts of risky conversations held sometimes over voice notes and sometimes in phone calls. His willingness to shed the skins he'd grown up in is the most shocking plot twist of my life. And like the alcoholic he once compared himself to, there is nothing I could have done to manipulate or force that change in him. Instead, he had to be the one to say and mean and choose to change for himself. Like I have to say and mean and choose to change for myself.

I'm thinking about this as I move one load of laundry over to the dryer and start another load in the washer. It's freezing outside. The kids are taking their end-of-semester tests early because we're flying out to South Africa for Christmas and pulling them out of school a week before it's officially closed for the holidays. The packing marathon has begun. Suitcases are dragged out from the deep recesses of closets and dusted off, and we discover that the zipper on one is broken just barely beyond use. Pete is determined to limit us all to one bag each this time, and I swear I haven't got it in me to go shopping for gifts we'll have to haul across the ocean, only to find myself a week later in the middle of Walmart and Costco trying to imagine what my teenage siblings would consider cool.

My phone is alive with voice notes from the South African family as we plan our time together, and it's been five years since all five of us Americans touched down in the Southern Hemisphere. My heart is racing and my middle kid is throwing up when we land. We're travel stained and jet-lagged as we disembark. And my firstborn, who was also born under South African skies, who took his first steps under the jacaranda tree outside my father's house and is now almost taller than me, wraps his arm around my shoulders and says, "We're home, Mom!" December is midsummer in South Africa, and from the moment we disembark, we can feel the warm air enveloping us, welcoming us back.

The line is long for noncitizens, and I wait with my adopted American passport in hand in the lane that makes me a foreigner on my native soil. I'm as nauseous and as excited as I was when I first left all those decades ago. I'm sweating and my stomach is turning over and over, and as we get to the front of the line, the immigration officer takes one look at me and says with compassion and my favorite accent, "Eish, you need a toilet, hey?" I nod and she scans my document and waves me through before she's finished with the rest of my family. I kneel in front of a toilet bowl, as humble a homecoming as I can imagine, while they pick up our bags, and then I meet them at customs. We walk through the line for those who have nothing to declare.

I have so much to declare. I want to declare my profound love for this place. This complicated, beautiful country that smells like big skies and dust and smoke from veld fires and fresh fruit and *braaivleis* and dry heat. This place and these people who have suffered and fought with each other and for each other and have been left behind by so many of us who left. So many are still here, writing stories that push back against violence, whether old or new. I am so proud to be related to some of them.

I want to declare my almost impossible tenderness toward my family who have been waiting for us for hours today and for years before that. One of my brothers has brought three of his little kids, and he's been entertaining them with views of the planes and the runway, since they arrived at seven A.M. to be sure they didn't miss our homecoming. I want to declare the warm blanket of gratitude toward my amazing stepmom, Wanda, who is the heartbeat of our family, the gravitational pull drawing children that span five decades all home, and who will be waiting, arm in arm with my dad. Oh, my dad. I want to declare that I am no longer afraid to go home to him. Love and grace and forgiveness have balanced out loss and pain and anger.

We are pushing two carts full of suitcases and backpacks and water bottles and gifts as we come around the corner into the arrivals hall, and the first thing I see are two of my nephews and one of my nieces all holding huge handmade signs reading, "Welcome Home Bakers!" And then I don't see anything properly anymore because my eyes are overwhelmed and my arms are full of my people and I'm down on my knees hugging the little ones, and then I'm in my father's arms and he smells like soft leather and sharp cologne and home. We're both crying and the first word I hear from him is my name. His voice that holds so much history in its accent wobbles with emotion: "Lisa-Jo. *Lisa-Jo!*" I feel his strength and also his years inside our hug. And I believe that the same God who was there at the beginning when Fritz prayed with my dad is standing with us now in the arrivals hall of Oliver Tambo International Airport holding our homecoming in His hands. He has always been working all things together toward this moment. He has always been making all things new.

* * *

There had been a summer afternoon in America when I sat on the carpet in my bedroom in Maryland and scared Peter by how hard I cried as I remembered all the ways my father's words had cut me. I traced the blue and brown and tan patterns in the carpet and asked Jesus if He even cared that once upon a time my father despised me enough to say that he spit in my face. That I can't stop the words from hurting no matter how far away I run. Then, it was as if I could almost hear Jesus say back, "Yes, I care. I care so much that I stood in front of you; I let him spit in My face instead of yours." The words had settled into my soul, warming some dark place buried there. I had sat with my head leaned back against the foot of my bed, all cried out, exhausted, and free as that thought slowly shifted two decades of weight off my chest.

And later, years later, my father had told me about a night when his pain of losing my mother, losing our farm, losing the hope of a second marriage, losing the church he saw as home, losing the life he saw as his birthright, poured out of him in a furious psalm-like prayer as he turned on God and demanded, "Do You know how I feel? Do You? Do You even care?"

And as he had sat on the floor of the house he'd traded up for after his first wife died, he told me he had heard the Father God's voice of deep understanding echo back through him in response: "I don't only know and care, but I feel your pain and I make your pain my own."

From opposite sides of the Atlantic Ocean my father and I have both gaped at the shocking statements that can be made only by a God who has lived a flesh-and-blood human life. A God who has felt the pain of estrangement, abandonment, ridicule, rejection, the death of a best friend, and the betrayal of another. A God so intimately familiar with pain that He can empathize with our human excruciating horrors from the inside out. This doesn't bring the people we love back into our living rooms; it doesn't cure the cancer in our bodies; it doesn't promise hollow happily ever afters. Instead, this is a God who bears witness to pain and promises to be with us through it until we arrive in His homeland, where pain can no longer follow. And when our pain is seen, recognized, acknowledged by such infinite tenderness and compassion, this makes way for the healing of forgiveness—the key to the lock on the door called freedom.

And as I stand in my father's arms, in a noisy arrivals hall, my throat still burning from my retching and my tears, surrounded by three generations of family all loudly speaking the language of love at the same time, surrounded by all our baggage, I bear witness to that truth.

We push our carts through the airport and into the parking lot and load up my parents' car, and I sit in the front seat and watch the horizon coming to greet me. I have lived in America now for most of my life. And yet, South Africa will always be my first home. She has formed me. She has shaped my language and, for better and worse, my ability to interpret the world. Like her, I am still learning.

We pull off the highway and turn into the neighborhood that bore witness to almost my entire adolescence. There is the gas station where I used to fill up my dad's car with petrol and my stomach with snacks. There is the row of flats where the Canadian pastor and his wife used to complain that we didn't call first before we dropped in. There is the church that refused to take us back and the primary school with the pool our high school borrowed, where a swimmer once showed me what it felt like to be loved. There is the grocery store and pharmacy and pizza place I've visited a hundred times with my Peter in tow. There is the hospital where we delivered our own firstborn into the world. And on the crest of a range of small hills sits my father's house, and as it comes into view, I can feel it pulling me home like gravity.

My most familiar memory of my dad is of him in his study at the top of that driveway, head bent over a Bible and a notebook, his desk lamp lighting the whole scene. The curtains are usually drawn against the late afternoon sun, and there's a photo of me from the year I left home on the wall above his desk. It is discolored now after years of hanging in direct sunlight. The pencil case with the special mirror inside it that he once gave my now twenty-one-year-old brother when he was four sits on his desk alongside flint arrowheads once found on our farm and a stack of prescription pads he still uses daily.

The room is lined with floor-to-ceiling bookshelves holding Bibles in countless languages, concordances, study guides, and stories of faith that span almost my father's entire life, from Middelburg to Cape Town to Zululand to Philadelphia to Pretoria. And if you're sitting in his leather chair that is cracked and peeling in patches after decades of use, you can see out the window to the jacaranda tree that presides over his house from its vantage point at the very top of the driveway. Every spring the tree drops a luxurious layer of purple trumpet petals that line the steep drive like a royal carpet that is irresistible to bees and risky for car tires, which lose all traction on the petals. And when my heart has been at its most homesick over the years, I can almost feel it throbbing from where I imagined burying it under that tree on the day I left home for America. Every year my dad considers cutting the tree down to reduce the risk of accidents and bee stings. But he holds off because he knows that part of my heart still lives in that tree.

Before we landed in Pretoria, my dad had phoned me from his study. Or more likely the call started in the study and then migrated with him upstairs to the kitchen—the heart of the house—with its second-floor view of the jacaranda, because I could hear teenagers coming and going in the background and Wanda stirring pots on the stove. Dinner prep was in full swing and my father was in midsentence when I heard Wanda say to him, "Tell her about the dream." My dad's voice came back half to her and half to me, "Um, yes, so *ja*, I can tell you about it. But it was a very short dream."

I'm instantly equal parts curious and anxious. Dreams have not always gone well for our family.

"I had been nervous about you coming home," I was surprised to hear my dad say. "Worried that it might not feel like it was worth your while, you know, to come so far. And maybe you guys would be disappointed in South Africa and us." My heart contracted as I listened, the family budgie chirping loudly in the background, my chest aching for my dad. But he went on, "I know how much you love jacaranda trees, Lisa-Jo. In my dream I saw all five of you and you were standing under a huge jacaranda, this jacaranda, your jacaranda, and it was in full flower. You were under a canopy so big it dwarfed the house with a rich shower of purple."

He finished the telling almost abruptly but we both lingered in the moment and I felt my heart burst wide open. After years of distance and pain and rage by both of us, toward

God and other people and each other and our children, Fritz's unembarrassed Jesus had been rearranging the architecture of my and my father's souls. The *Groot Geneser,* the Great Healer, had always been working to remake the parts of my father and me that had been malformed by our childhoods. To teach us a new language to pass on to the next generation. And the tree and the house I once ran away from had blossomed into a sacred, safe place to return to.

The car turns onto our street and swings wide to fit its heavy girth up our steep, narrow driveway. My kids are craning their necks back for a good first look at the home they've almost forgotten, this house that sits at the top of a steep hill, built into the side of the rocks, in the shade of a jacaranda tree. My dad had named his house. In the in-between years, when he was healing and his family was expanding and his oldest daughter was still stranded overseas, he named it Honeyrock. Named for the beehives behind the house and the rocks beneath it. If you were talking to him, he'd have more layers of meaning to share. But for me, the name is interpreted against the backdrop of my own experiences with the house. For me, I see Samson, the most violent of all God's judges, who fought a lion and killed it with his bare hands. And later discovered that bees had made their home in its carcass, spinning life and honey out of death and decay. I hear Samson's riddle in my mind:

Out of the eater, something to eat;
out of the strong, something sweet. (Judges 14:14, NIV)

The heavy car groans as it passes the house number and name nailed to an old bit of driftwood, and I think about how

Honeyrock used to terrify me with its roaring pain. But now, when we pull up its steep driveway and park in the shade of its purple tree, the next generation spilling out of the house with hugs and hollers of welcome, my father unloading my suitcase and holding my hand, I discover a sweetness so tender it tastes like grace.

ACKNOWLEDGMENTS

Dad—you are my favorite storyteller. Thank you for trusting me with this story, your story, *our* story. You have modeled a kind of parenting courage and vulnerability I will never forget. May I be able to pass this on to my own children with your kind of humility. For years you were both mom and dad to me. My very own Mr. Mom. Your story is the reason that on the days that doubts threaten to overwhelm me I will still always believe in the truth of Jesus. I know no other way to explain your life than the God who is always patiently making all things new—fathers and daughters, countries and stories. I love you, my dad. Thank you for how you have loved me with your words and your actions. And for how you read every page of this book and for every voice note you left me with your tender and careful feedback. This was a sacred space to share with you. Thank you for being willing to remember with me. The hard and the holy, the painful, the broken, and the beautiful. From our first conversation about the monster in our story five years ago to the final pages of this book. You have never once put up your defenses. You have welcomed me home with words and actions and airplane tickets and car rides and conversations. This is our story and I'm honored to share it with you. Thank you for bravely letting me leave home and more bravely living a life that welcomed me back again.

Wanda—thank you for putting our family back together and for being the superglue that keeps us all coming home again. Mama and *Ouma*—your fierce love is always teaching me more about how parenting never quits and how to be generous with time, with adventures, with memory making, with babysitting, with kitchen dance parties and dates with our teenagers, with believing the best of the kids God brings into our lives and being a safe harbor, a Cape of Good Hope, for the next generation.

To my big, little brothers, Joshua and Luke. You have both outgrown me in so many ways. We share scars and now we also share a story of healing—physically and spiritually. I look up to you both now in faith and forgiveness, in joy and do-overs. I'll never forget being in your homes on that October trip, you know the one, and the holy ground of remembering together and forgiving together. Thank you for speaking the language of love with me, to me, and over me. I'm so glad we all tell stories for a living, like our mom. We have shared some good ones. I look forward to the ones still coming.

To my middle brother and sister, Jonty and Ann. I'm so glad we share our special parental unit. What a family we have! You two have taught me, even from a distance, what it looks like to become blood brothers and sisters with people who aren't our blood. Thank you for the gift of your mom and for loving my dad. This is a family that just keeps getting better.

To my little brother and sisters, Ben Karabo, Lia, Lulu, and Mo. You came into our lives at the same time Pete and I became parents, and watching you guys and our guys all grow up together is a whole new level of joy. There's nothing like this new bond, and you four are the reason it's absolutely terrible every time we have to leave South Africa. Thank you for breaking our hearts with homesickness. Thank you for sharing bedrooms and computer games, rondavels and workouts, meals and memories, baseball caps and car trips, dance tunes and FaceTimes. Your house is our house and our house is your house, and you owe us a trip this side!

To the extended Baker and Rous families and all the branches of our family tree with different last names. Thank you for making room for a writer in this family. I know it's risky business. I don't take your trust or your advice or your encouragement lightly.

To Lisa Jackson, my agent. It took me more than a decade, but I finally wrote the book you signed me for so long ago. Thank you for believing in it long before I did. Thank you for the hours of messages back and forth, the patience with my fear, the faith in my ability. Thank you for hanging with me so long in the in-between years. For being my champion, my first reader, my biggest fan, and, most important, my friend.

To Christie Purifoy, you have traveled the whole long road of this book with me. How can the words "thank you" possibly hold all the tears cried and rewrites championed and plot threads brainstormed? Thank you for seeing the road ahead when I couldn't and telling me it was worth it to keep going.

To Ann Voskamp, for holding sacred space for my fear, my sorrow, my shame, my tears, and my doubts as I've tried to piece this book and my life together the past five years. Thank you for always picking up the phone. Thank you for always listening. Thank you for always preaching hope into the darkest parts of my life. Thank you for holding my grief in Canada and in Utah on the darkest days of the other journey I was on.

Thank you for always, always showing me the Way and for never once not telling me how much you believed in my writing.

To my first tender readers, Kate Motaung and Quanny Ard. Thank you for your time, your wisdom, your insights, and your encouragement.

To the women whose voices have preached truth and encouragement in my head in the dark hours of putting these stories on the page—thank you for being a lighthouse. You can't possibly know how many times I replayed your messages or reread your texts or emails. Alinda Mashiku, Becky Keife, Becky Kopitzke, Elise Hurd, Emily Graffius, Jennifer Dukes Lee, Katie Reid, Kristen Strong, and Shannan Martin. I am in your encouragement debt.

To my Green Chair Sisters, Lynn Brooks and Lorene Huffman. Thank you for holding holy ground with me—whether on the floor of Lynn's office, my shed, Sunday school classrooms, or your kitchens. Thank you for a thousand prayers and listening to me rail about the impossibility of this project for a thousand hours. Thank you for believing, bringing Starbucks, and making regular dinner dates. You are family to me.

To my South African childhood friends, Dorothy, Liza, and Rozanna. I'm so grateful the ties that started so long ago still hold. We have shared so many pivotal moments in this growing-up journey. Crushes and first kisses, cancer and chemo, death and coming of age, driver's licenses, late nights dancing, Sunday school, degrees and overseas travel, the language of childhood and home. It's sacred to me that I still get to call you friends. We may live on three different continents now, but we'll never not still be the matric class from Willow-ridge of 1992. I'm so grateful to always have that in common with you three.

To my editor, Keren Baltzer. You were the toughest writing coach I've always wanted. If this book were football training, I would have been throwing up on the sidelines at almost every grueling practice. Thank you for pushing me every time I thought I was done. Thank you for making me a better writer. Thank you for your patience with this project. I'm so glad you took me on.

To the team at Convergent, thank you for caring for this project that you inherited and for helping me across the finish line. Your care for the writing and the cover and your creativity in getting this story into the world is something that means the world to a writer with a shrinking platform. Thank you for adopting me so fully.

To the team at WaterBrook & Multnomah, especially Susan Tjaden and Laura Barker, for the extension of incredible grace time and again as this book morphed and was reimagined and as the deadline came and went several times over several years. The space you gave me to figure this out was invaluable as an author. And rare. Thank you for that gift.

To my church, Crossroads Church of the Nazarene, thank you for being more than a building, but for also offering me practical space in your building during the pandemic, when I was trying to write and work and juggle three kids and their full-time school from home. To be welcomed in to write about the work God has done in our family in the same place where I worship that same God is nothing short of the sweetest kind of testimony to what church can be—family and home, calling and worship.

To the musicians who were the soundtrack of my childhood and this book, thank you for being some of my favorite teachers, turning truth and pain, celebration and sorrow, into harmony and collective memory: Joseph Shabalala and Ladysmith Black Mambazo, Mango Groove, Spokes Mashiyane, Johnny Clegg & Savuka, Vusi Mahlasela, Freshly Ground, Ndlovu Youth Choir, Soweto Gospel Choir, Mafikizolo, Jeremy Loops, Lucky Dube, Eddy Grant, Miriam Makeba, and Bright Blue.

To my children, Jackson, Micah, and Zoe. You had a mother who was locked up in writing and editing for years, and you three were the best kind of cheerleaders. Thank you for all the nights you asked me how it was going, hugged me as I ranted and railed about how impossible it was, and kept believing I would, one day, finally finish. Thank you for making me laugh late at night, talking me into just one more episode of whatever you were watching, and never taking me too seriously. I'm honored to entrust this story to you. I love that South Africa is as much yours as it is mine. Sorry not sorry for the homesickness you've inherited from me. You are my favorite people to travel with, and I love seeing the world and our family through your eyes. Keep rolling your windows down. Never stop asking questions. You make me and Dad prouder than anything else we've ever done. Please keep coming home no matter where you move away to one day. I promise to always make you *melktert*.

To my husband and best friend, Peter. Your mind is still my favorite place to visit. Your arms my favorite place to laugh. You have carried me and our family through the last three years. It was a Herculean task—how you lifted pretty much every single scrap of the family admin, driving, shopping, cooking, planning, and parenting off my shoulders so I could write and write and write alongside my full-time job while you were still juggling yours! Thank you for being part of this marathon. Writing is a team sport, and I can't fathom how I would have managed it without you in my corner. Thank you for everything—even wielding a pen and, true to form, marking up the pages of this manuscript. Without fail, you still have my favorite arms and editorial suggestions.

Jesus—thank You for the story You've written in our family. Thank You that You are the God who makes all things new. Not fixed. Not the same. Not even how we might have hoped. But new. Thank You for giving me this glimpse of the end of the story You always knew was coming while we were all still at the beginning. Thank You for never forgetting to circle back to plot points that I never thought would be resolved. Thank You for making me and my family new. Always beautifully, wildly, unexpectedly new. *Ngiyabonga Jesu.*

NOTES

Chapter 1: Family Thorn Tree

1. Tony Fawcett, "Success for Mallee Dorper Saltbush Lamb," *Weekly Times*, November 11, 2013, www.weeklytimesnow.com .au/agribusiness/on-farm/success-for-mallee-dorper-saltbush -lamb/news-story/36ec00539628a9001fdf57621cf2ba28.

Chapter 2: Tea and Baboons

1. *Dictionary of South African English*, s.v. "nonnie," https://dsae .co.za/entry/nonnie/e05237.
2. "Blue Italian," Spode History, www.spode.com/spode -collections-blue-italian.
3. Pam Woolliscroft, "Spode and Italian Pattern," Spode History, December 29, 2010, https://spodehistory.blogspot .com/2010/12/italian-pattern.html.
4. Pam Woolliscroft, "Spode and Chinese Rose," Spode History, August 8, 2011, https://spodehistory.blogspot.com/2011/08 /chinese-rose-pattern.html.

Chapter 3: 1984

1. David Crary, "Monitoring Group Says 8,000 Children Detained Since June with AM-South Africa," AP News, November 27, 1986, apnews.com/article/3bdc8dcb220c0c98a0ceae7dc424546f. In 1984, our country would begin a brutal and systematic response to the anti-apartheid movement that would culminate in two nationwide states of emergency in 1985 and 1986. The ruthless special branch of the South African police force, unre-

strained by the need for warrants, would launch predawn raids and seize students, school kids, pastors, priests, musicians, and activists alike, along with nearly the entire leadership of the United Democratic Front, the main anti-apartheid coalition. Of the approximately twenty thousand people held without warrants or charges, about eight thousand were schoolchildren. See also: Times Wire Services, "Botha Imposes Nationwide Emergency; U.S. Protests: Hundreds Seized in Roundup." *Los Angeles Times*, June 12, 1986, www.latimes.com/archives/la-xpm-1986 -06-12-mn-10542-story.html.

2. Times Wire Services, "Botha Imposes Nationwide Emergency; U.S. Protests: Hundreds Seized in Roundup," *Los Angeles Times*, June 12, 1986, www.latimes.com/archives/la-xpm-1986-06-12 -mn-10542-story.html.

3. Times Wire Services, "Botha Imposes Nationwide Emergency."

4. "Bishop Desmond Tutu leaves for the USA to meet with American President Ronald Reagan," South African History Online, December 7, 1984, www.sahistory.org.za/dated-event/bishop -desmond-tutu-leaves-usa-meet-american-president-ronald -reagan.

5. Times Wire Services, "Botha Imposes Nationwide Emergency."

6. Will Dunham, "'Karoo Firewalkers': Dinosaurs Braved South Africa's Land of Lava," Reuters, January 29, 2020, www.reuters .com/article/us-science-footprints/karoo-firewalkers-dinosaurs -braved-south-africas-land-of-lava-idUSKBN1ZS2XS.

7. In a unique twist, Jozua Naudé's son, Beyers Naudé, would eventually reject his father's ideology and become a significant voice in the anti-apartheid struggle. Allister Sparks, "Once Afrikaner Paragon, Conscientious Churchman Now Pariah," *Washington Post*, November 5, 1982, www.washingtonpost.com /archive/politics/1982/11/05/once-afrikaner-paragon -conscientious-churchman-now-pariah/8f39fb4b-1292-4369-818c -43b996f30a06/.

8. "Fossielen en sedimenten," Paleontica Foundation, www .paleontica.org/article/77/Fossielen_en_sedimenten.

Chapter 7: Coming to America

1. Facing History & Ourselves, "Introduction: Early Apartheid: 1948–1970," last updated August 3, 2018. www.facinghistory .org/resource-library/introduction-early-apartheid-1948-1970.

Chapter 8: Roll Down Your Window

1. Joseph Lelyveld, "Pretoria's Whites Preparing for Decades of Conflict with Black Insurgents," *New York Times,* October 11, 1983, www.nytimes.com/1983/10/11/world/pretoria-s-whites -preparing-for-decades-of-conflict-with-black-insurgents .html.

Chapter 9: What Our Scars Mean

1. "The Mason-Dixon Line History," www.thomaslegion.net /themasondixonlinehistory.html.

Chapter 11: Tourists

1. Felicity Spector, "The Power of Forgiveness: Mandela's Legacy to the World," Channel 4 News, December 6, 2013, www .channel4.com/news/the-power-of-forgiveness-mandelas -legacy-to-the-world.

2. Teresa Godwin Phelps, *Shattered Voices: Language, Violence, and the Work of Truth Commissions* (Philadelphia: University of Pennsylvania Press, 2004).

3. Years later I would look up the official report from that day. While the town has since been renamed Polokwane (meaning "Place of Safety" in Sesotho), the TRC report and transcript from that day has it listed by its old name, along with the names of all fourteen amnesty applicants. It also contains the transcript of the stories we listened to that day: PIETERSBURG—1 (June 30–July 4, 1997). The transcripts from the applicants and the witnesses are available here: www.justice.gov.za/trc /amntrans/am1997.htm. The final report with the commis-

sion's findings is here: https://sabctrc.saha.org.za/documents/decisions/58782.htm.

4. From the testimony of one of the fathers of the victims, Mr. Moloi. "Amnesty Hearing: Stephan C. F. Moloi," South African Truth and Reconciliation Commission, Department of Justice, March 7, 1997, www.justice.gov.za/trc/amntrans/pburg/moloi.htm.

5. "Amnesty Hearing: Stephan C. F. Moloi."

6. From the testimony of one of the mothers of the victims, Mrs. Moloi. "Amnesty Hearing: Stephan C. F. Moloi."

7. SABC News, "Amnesty Decisions," Truth Commission Special Report, April 15, 1999, https://sabctrc.saha.org.za/documents/decisions/58782.htm.

8. Tanni Deb and Segun Akande, "Inside Ghana's Elmina Castle Is a Haunting Reminder of Its Grim Past," CNN, July 30, 2018, www.cnn.com/2018/07/27/africa/ghana-elmina-castle.

9. "1994 Election," Apartheid Museum, www.apartheidmuseum.org/exhibitions/1994-election.

10. "The South African General Elections: 1994," South African History Online, www.sahistory.org.za/article/south-african-general-elections-1994.

About the Author

Lisa-Jo Baker is a bestselling author of *Never Unfriended, Surprised by Motherhood,* and *The Middle Matters.* With a BA in English/prelaw from Gordon College and a JD from the University of Notre Dame Law School, Baker has lived and worked on three continents in the human rights field. Her writings have resonated with thousands and have been featured on *HuffPost, BibleGateway,* Fox News, Today.com, *Christianity Today,* and more. A sought-after national speaker, she is the co-host of the *Out of the Ordinary* podcast. Originally from South Africa, Baker now lives with her family just outside Washington, D.C.

lisajobaker.com
outoftheordinarypodcast.com
facebook.com/lisajobaker
Instagram: @lisajobaker

ABOUT THE TYPE

This book was set in Dante, a typeface designed by Giovanni Mardersteig (1892–1977). Conceived as a private type for the Officina Bodoni in Verona, Italy, Dante was originally cut only for hand composition by Charles Malin, the famous Parisian punch cutter, between 1946 and 1952. Its first use was in an edition of Boccaccio's *Trattatello in laude di Dante* that appeared in 1954. The Monotype Corporation's version of Dante followed in 1957. Though modeled on the Aldine type used for Pietro Cardinal Bembo's treatise *De Aetna* in 1495, Dante is a thoroughly modern interpretation of that venerable face.

Available from
LISA-JO BAKER

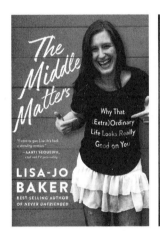

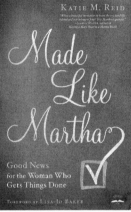

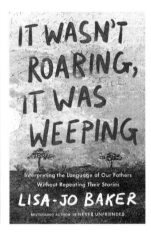